KEITH TUMA is the author of *Fishing by Obstinate Isles: Modern and Postmodern British Poetry and American Readers* (Northwestern, 1998) and editor of *Anthology of Twentieth-Century British and Irish Poetry* (Oxford, 2001). He teaches at Miami University in Ohio.

KEITH TUMA

ON LEAVE

*a book of
anecdotes*

SALT

LONDON

PUBLISHED BY SALT PUBLISHING
Acre House, 11-15 William Road, London NW1 3ER,
United Kingdom

Printed in the United States by Lightning Souce Inc

Typeset in Bembo 12 / 13.5

ISBN 978 1 84471 486 5 paperback

1 3 5 7 9 8 6 4 2

for Diane

i.m. Marilyn Tuma and Pascale Redding Chow

Contents

ON
LEAVE

Introduction

Near the beginning of *Nadja* (1928), André Breton writes that criticism would do well to abandon its "dearest prerogatives" for "a goal less futile than the automatic adjustment of ideas." In Breton's view, changes in standards of taste or literary value, as also in literary practice, are not importantly shaped by criticism. Instead of passing judgment upon works, critical writing about literature and art would do better to "explore the very realm supposedly barred to it, and which, separate from the work, is a realm where the author's personality, victimized by the petty events of daily life, expresses itself quite freely and often in so distinctive a manner." Breton hoped that efforts to write about authors in everyday, extra-literary contexts would replace what his generation knew as criticism—Adorno would have called it "cultural criticism" and despised it for the "dazzled and arrogant recognition" it seeks to confer upon culture.

It is not full-length biography that Breton has in mind but rather the biographical anecdote. Offering an example of what he hopes for from commentary, Breton relays an anecdote about Victor Hugo and his mistress Juliette Drouet riding in their carriage. The two ride past an estate featuring two gates. Hugo points to the larger of the gates:

> Hugo, for perhaps the thousandth time, would say: "Bridle gate, Madame," to which Juliette, pointing to the small gate, would reply: "Pedes-

trian gate, Monsieur"; then, a little farther on, passing two trees with intertwining branches, Hugo would remark: "Philemon and Baucis," knowing that Juliette would not answer; we have reason to believe that this marvelous, poignant ritual was repeated daily for years on end; yet how could the best possible study of Hugo's work give us a comparable awareness, the astonishing sense of what he was, of what he is? Those two gates are like the mirror of his strength and his weakness, we do not know which stands for his insignificance, which for his greatness. And what good would all the genius in the world be to us if it failed to countenance that adorable correction, the redress of love itself, which so perfectly characterizes Juliette's reply? The subtlest, the most enthusiastic of Hugo's critics will never make me feel anything to equal this supreme sense of *proportion*. I should be privileged indeed to possess, in the case of each of the men I admire, a personal document of corresponding value.

Breton's phrase "this supreme sense of proportion" means to describe the conversation of Hugo and Drouet and the rest of their "poignant ritual." Does it also refer to aesthetic values that shape Hugo's work and might be found in it? Breton ignores the ambiguity, promoting a view of Hugo and Hugo's writing that finds something essential in this vignette, this perfect anecdote. The two gates are symbols of the strength and weakness of Hugo's work, but Breton won't say which is which.

Breton also values what is usually called table talk. He is fascinated by glimpses of the author and the author's offhand remarks. The translation again is by Richard Howard:

> Lacking these [i.e., personal documents], I should even be content with records of a lesser value, less self-contained from an emotional point of view. I do not admire Flaubert, yet when I am told that by his own admission all he hoped to accomplish in *Salammbô* was to "give the impression of the color yellow," and in *Madame Bovary* "to do something that would have the color of those mouldy cornices that harbor wood lice," and that he cared for nothing else, such generally extra-literary preoccupations leave me anything but indifferent.

Image does the work explanation *might* do: the phrase "mouldy cornices that harbor wood lice" probably suggests the moral and emotional rot that Flaubert's novel explores, but how can we know that for certain? An anecdotal criticism might be a more *poetic* criticism.

Breton would have us fold the most mundane extra-literary information into exegesis of the artistic or literary work:

> The magnificent light in Courbet's paintings is for me the same as that of the Place Vendôme, at the time the Column fell. If today a man like Chirico would confide—entirely and, of course, artlessly, including the least consequential as well as the most disturbing details—what it was that once made him paint as he did, such a step, taken by such a man, would mean an enormous advance for exegesis.

There is little about Breton's sense of the value of the extra-literary in exegesis that is controversial; the extra-literary has a secure place in the academic study of literature. Texts and contexts blur, cross and proliferate in cultural studies and elsewhere. But Breton's anecdotes are exceptional for working so hard to avoid being absorbed by other discourses that would put them to use. They want their own life.

The thing about the best anecdotal criticism is that it cannot be reduced to method or system. It values style above argument, allows impression equal footing with knowledge. The greatest anecdotalist among recent literary critics, Hugh Kenner, wrote in a manner that has had few imitators.

⌒

Over the years I have written about a scattering of poems authored by poets I have met. I have not written about the poets who are responsible for these poems, certainly not about the poets as persons. I have tried to do a little of that here with recourse to sources no more reliable than memory and hearsay. I have tried to write a book of anecdotes about my poet friends, with the hope that they will still be my friends after they read it.

Questions emerged as soon as I began. Did I want to write anecdotes aspiring to the vividness of Breton's anecdote about Hugo and Drouet? Of course. Did I want also to demonstrate—to explain—ways that anecdotes might help a reader understand specific poems, or the practice of a specific poet, or something about the poetry world? These questions persisted throughout the writing as background doubt. They were accompanied by lots of questions having to do with the risks and challenges of representing persons rather than poems, even when the purpose is to remember, to honor.

I use the word "story" in what follows more or less interchangeably with "anecdote," but it was the anecdote rather than the story that interested me, as I imagined that it might have a more specific or definable form. I was probably wrong about that. What I knew about the anecdote, the literary anecdote, before I started, was what everybody knows: anecdotes are short. Some years earlier I'd written a one-page account of a visit by the poet Tom Raworth as part of a tribute published for his 60th birthday, and I thought it included a glimpse of Raworth that might interest readers of his poetry. It was compact—that was the important thing. I thought that the brevity and more or less self-contained nature of the anecdote would allow me to set modest goals for writing during my leave of absence from my work as chair of an English department, and to stick with them: I'd try to bang out one anecdote at each sitting. It soon occurred to me that it was likely that I didn't have a sufficient supply of anecdotes, or anyway not of anecdotes I wanted to preserve, to keep me occupied for the whole year. I also thought I would need some way of organizing the anecdotes in a book. So I decided to keep a daybook that would follow the year and allow me to write about some of what was happening during my year on leave, as it happened. A few poets were scheduled to come through town. I would mix accounts of their visits with anecdotes about the past as I remembered them.

Not all daybooks are alike. Some have room for introspection. I had in mind books like Hannah Weiner's *Weeks* and Peter Manson's *Adjunct: An*

Undigest—not daybooks exactly, to be sure, certainly not daybooks much interested in meditative prose, but instead works of experimental writing heavily invested in fact and event. I admire the ways both writers chronicle quotidian experience. Parataxis in their works allows them to represent events without worrying about folding them into story or commenting at any length. Manson's book apparently owes the ordering of its sentences to the randomizing influence of a computer program. *Weeks* is closer to what I wanted to try to write because the procedures guiding its composition more closely resemble those of the traditional journal or daybook, which is to say that the book follows the calendar, whatever else it does with its materials. In his introduction to the Xexoxial edition, Charles Bernstein describes Weiner's book:

> *Weeks* was written in a small notebook, one page per day for fifty weeks. Every page of the book is the equivalent of a single week, with each day taking its toll in about five lines. The material, says Weiner, is all found—"taken at the beginning from written matter and TV news and later almost entirely from TV news."

I like it that Weiner's method helps her turn down "the lyrical interference of the ego," to cite Charles Olson's famous phrase, though that is not a program I feel obliged to sign on to here or elsewhere. I also had less interest in writing something that provides critical perspective on the "self-enclosed artifacts that we call news," to quote another part of Bernstein's introduction, as the fact that the news requires a critical perspective is hardly news. I did want to incorporate "the found" as I could, to help keep track of the time.

It might help to have a little of Weiner's text here to see the model I had in front of me—though I had no intention of compressing my writing to the point that it would aspire to the condition of poetry. I won't try to duplicate the look of the page in the Xexoxial edition:

Sips of morning coffee alternate with bits of crackers and jam
Film Forum announces an evening with Yevgeny Yevtushenko
Concerts of sixteenth century music for lute don't happen often
The yahrtzeit for my Aunt Reka is Shevat 3, next Monday
Dial the weather for the temperature   I have just finished reading
Harvard Magazine   On the way to the Dr. to get a shot   Residential
Continuing Care Retirement Community for those who wish to live
life to its fullest   Limousine and driver, cook, housekeeping,
baby sitter, tour guide   Breakfast is over   A long letter from
Pete Spence from Oct or Nov is on the table   So are the books
he sent, Quilt, Some-One, Skywriter, and Handwritten Modern
Classic and some promo material from Sybella, a cooperative press
in Australia   A new law bans mandatory retirement   I ate eleven
crackers to average out with yesterday's thirteen   Today is the
day to wash my hair   Writing that goes beyond traditional ideas
political arena moves to the streets   I rarely invent anything
to say   Boustrophedon (bústrofidan) as the ox turns in plowing—
refers to writing from left to right and then reversing direction
to continue writing now right to left   Yes, the window installation
process is a pain in the _____   Reading the owner's newsletter ...

Bernstein is right that Weiner's parataxis "takes on an ominous tone in its refusal to draw connections." For my project, I viewed hers and related practices as a kind of upper limit for compression, while leaving room for other, more leisurely forms of chronicling experience, and, now and again, even for a little musing. To be truthful I had nothing like a system, no procedure with rigorous guidelines, only the desire to write regularly, and to do so in modular units that would free me from the imperative to develop and link thoughts and observations. I hoped the anecdotes

I could remember would form the core of a larger book.

⁓

We owe one of the *OED*'s definitions of "anecdote" to the Byzantine historian Procopius and his *Secret History*, otherwise known as the *Anecdota*. "Secret history" suggests his book's contents, its unsparing account of the "contemptible conduct" of Theodora, Justinian, and the general Belisarius, key figures among a sixth-century Byzantine elite. Procopius might have been from Constantinople, but constant he was not: *Secret History* trashes the very same people he flatters in his longer, more tedious books, histories of the empire that few bother to read. G. A. Williamson, the translator of the Penguin Classics edition, details the history of the title:

> The title by which it is usually known suits it well enough, but is of late Latin origin and bears no resemblance to the Greek title, for which likewise the author was not responsible. The Greeks called it the *Anecdota*, which Gibbon misleadingly translated 'Anecdotes.' The word *Anecdota*, which was applied to it by the lexicographer Suidas, means 'Unpublished things,' and was used because the book was not published in the author's lifetime.

Our modern sense of the anecdote as "a brief account of a humorous or interesting incident," to cite the definition offered by one online dictionary, seems to have taken hold only in the eighteenth century. This is more or less the meaning of the word for Boswell and Dr. Johnson. Marvell and Swift use "anecdote" in the older sense of "secret history" or "unpublished things."

Scholars of classical literature and rhetoric point to *chreia* (from the Greek "chreiodes," which means "useful") as the Greek antecedent of our contemporary anecdote. Marion C. Moeser takes her definition of *chreia* from Theon of Alexandria: "A *Chreia* is a concise and pointed account of something said or done, attributed to some particular person." In her study of the continuities and discontinuities between Lucian's *Demonax* and the Christian Gospel of Mark, and between these works and the rabbinic writing of the Mishnah, Moeser describes three types of *chreia* that Theon gives examples for—narratives containing a saying, narratives containing an action, and narratives containing an action and a saying. All include a setting for the brief account or narrative, for the anecdote. Surveying definitions of the anecdote, Moeser offers her own: "a brief narrative, either oral or written, describing an incident, including its setting, which involves one or more persons and which focuses on an action, saying, or dialogue; the function of an anecdote is to entertain, instruct, relate an historical incident, characterize a person, or authoritatively legitimate a specific opinion, a specific practice, or a broader view of reality." Moeser's definition works hard to cover all bases and describes not only the form but also the function of the anecdote. She acknowledges that her definition does not cover all that has been *called* an anecdote or collected as such.

The literary scholars who are called New Historicists, Joel Fineman especially, hoped that strategic use of the anecdote might promote "counter-history," a mode of literary historiography that resists the causal

9

explanation and teleology characteristic of older forms of historicism. For these critics and literary historians the anecdote is a "*petit récit*" that might "puncture the historical *grand récit* into which it [is] inserted," as Catherine Gallagher and Stephen Greenblatt write in discussing Fineman's work. Anecdotes are "complete little stories unto themselves" for Gallagher and Greenblatt, but they aren't especially interested in the anecdote as a genre; they are concerned with the *use* of the anecdote. The anecdote, Fineman wrote, "produces the effect of the real, the occurrence of contingency, by establishing an event as an event within and yet without the framing context of historical successivity." Much as Breton's anecdote about Hugo resists interpretation, anecdotes not subsumed by causal explanation offer literary history (or "counter-history") the density of the literary work. The New Historicists hoped that the anecdote would thicken literary history, and that seemed, and still seems, a worthwhile goal.

As I came to know a little more about what has been written about anecdotes, I learned that one scholar, the historian Lionel Gossman, has suggested that anecdotes have something in common with *faits divers*, the French news stories or news filler that Félix Fénéon raised to the status of avant-garde literature in his *Nouvelles en trois lignes*. I am not sure how far to follow Gossman in suggesting a resemblance; the anecdote is much harder to bring into focus. Here is one of Fénéon's stories, in Luc Sante's translation: "The sinister prowler seen by the mechanic Gicquel near Herblay train station has been identified: Jules Ménard, snail collector." Sante notes that the French have been "clipping and saving" news stories like the ones this prose is based on "for their oddity or their usually unintentional humor . . . since the *fait-divers* first made its appearance in the nineteenth century." But the joke in this little story is clearly intentional, the sentence in Sante's translation perfect for the way it withholds its crucial information, its punch line, until the end: Ménard is hunting for snails rather than prowling with evil intentions. In the end, the anecdote is not as recognizable a form as the *fait divers* and therefore not so ripe for pastiche and parody. As a category of writing, it is just baggy, the efforts of Moeser and others notwithstanding. The anecdote is short on plot, and anecdotes often relay odd, unusual, or previously undisclosed facts, so the comparison makes some sense, but the *fait divers* seems a culturally specific form.

As far as plot goes, Louis Brownlow writes in his *The Anatomy of the Anecdote* (1960), "The anecdote does demand the classic unity of a beginning, a middle, and an end, but it finds its beginning in the memories and minds of its hearers, devises no plot for its middle and, therefore, needs no dénouement for its end. For its end it needs only the jolt of 'finis'—with sometimes a little after-play for savor." This makes most sense if we understand the anecdote as belonging to storytelling. (As we see in Moeser's definition, the anecdote is not only an oral form.) The anecdote, for Brownlow, depends upon knowledge of character and backstory. You know such and such a poet already, but have you heard this? As for the "jolt" and the "after-play"—well, there are good anecdotes and not so good anecdotes. Brownlow, his Aristotle in hand, works a little too hard at definition, like Moeser but to different ends. Anecdotes are a base material for other genres, and thus it is no surprise really that there has been comparatively little interest in defining something essential to them, or that it is difficult to do so.

This is more than I knew or wanted to know about anecdotes when I started my project. I knew then only that I was interested in daily writing and intended to pursue that writing by working in modular units of prose. With an open plan like that, and following my nose, I came to investigate what has counted or might count as an anecdote, and what a few writers have said about anecdotes, "literary" anecdotes in particular, and what others besides Breton have done with the anecdote in critical or exegetical writing. I read collections of anecdotes that libraries buy and nobody reads, certainly never cover to cover. This kind of collection goes back a ways, back beyond *The Percy Anecdotes*, a collection originally published in 40 installments over 40 months beginning in 1820, near the end of what was arguably the golden age of the literary anecdote.

The Percy Anecdotes, which has since gone through many editions, contains anecdotes collected and edited by Reuben Percy (Thomas Byerley) and Sholto Percy (Joseph Clinton Robertson). The online edition available at http://www.mspong.org/percy/index.htm includes a preface identifying Lord Byron as an enthusiastic reader of the anecdotes. It features "historical gossip" and was primarily "intended for the innocent tastes of a large class of readers," to cite the online preface. Here is the list of entries for Eloquence, one category for the anecdotes gathered in the book, which includes an anecdote about a speech by the most famous ancestor of the contemporary English poet J.H. Prynne:

Extemporaneous Oratory
Demosthenes
Isocrates
Pericles
Plato
Public Criers of Greece
Cicero
Prolixity made Penal
Mark Antony, the Consul
Hortensius
Hortensia
Funeral Orations
Boadicea
Crillon - King Clovis
Peter the Hermit
Pope Urban II
Massillon
John Knox
Bossuet
Saurin
Dr. Barrow
Independence of the Bar
Cromwell's Chaplain
The Long Parliament
Audi Alteram Partem
Fletcher of Salton
Earl of Shaftesbury
Royal Commissioner
Bishop Merks
Queen Elizabeth
Margaret Lambrun
Sir Nicholas Throckmorton
Long Speeches

Earl of Carnarvon
Reporters
Jeremy Taylor, Bishop of Down. I
Bishop Atterbury
Logan, the Indian
Philip, Duke of Wharton
Frederic the Great
Sir Thomas Sewell
Patrick Henry
Tecumseh
Lord Loughborough
Effect
Physiognomy
Edward IV
French Curate
Flechier
Tillotson
Bishop Porteus
Excommunication
Quaker Preaching
The Rival Orators
Hottentot Preaching
Caractacus
Lord Belhaven
Naval Oratory
Lord Duncan
Lord Chatham
Death of Lord Chatham
Royal Elocution
Mr. Burke
David Hartley
Single-speech Hamilton
Burke and Fox
Pitt and Sheridan
Lord Ellenborough
Mr. Windham
Parliamentary Courtier of 1626
Last Days of Knox
Pulpit Flattery Re-

proved
Parliament of Paris
Mahomet
Giorgio Scali
Impeachment of the Earl of Strafford
Magdaleine de Savoie
Fisher, Bishop of Rochester
Henry IV. of France
Extraordinary Inspiration
Prynn's Speech on the Scaffold
Pulteney, first Earl of Bath
Sir John Bernard
Mr. Sheridan
Quarrel between Flood and Grattan
The Begum Charge
Lord Erskine
Mr. Fox's India Bill
Sir Elijah Impey
The Chicken
Themistocles
A Hint well Taken
Quin
Church Militants
Parliament of 1794
Parliamentary Literature
The Thread of Discourse
Doctor Shawl
Way to Promotion
The Orator and the Tyrant
Pirate's Defence
Bold Appeal
Hannibal
Whitfield

L. Sylla
Demetrius
The Dagger
The Orator of the
    Human Race
Political Friendships
Power of Elocution
Venetian Mounte-
    bank
Law Latin
Judge Foster
Doctor Hussey
Lord Mansfield
Jesuit of Maranham
Lord Thurlow
A 'Fierce Democ-
    racy.'
Venetian Pleading
Eloquence of
    Silence
Soldiers' Appeal
Royal Favour

Earl of Peterbor-
    ough
Sir Richard Pepper
    Arden
Bench and Bar -
    their Duties
Symbolical Oratory
Candid Beggar
Oratorical Experi-
    ment
Graces of Speech
Athenian Orators
Philip alla the Athe-
    nian Orators
Freedom of Speech
Facetious Preachers
Catholic Missionary
A Base Brief Hon-
    ourably Refused
Sir Samuel Romilly
Frederic the Great
Heroic Negro
The Gift of Tongues

Time and Eternity
Perfumery Taxes
Jewel, Bishop of
    Salisbury
Kirwan, Dean of
    Killaloe
Free-spoken Ambas-
    sador
The Earl of Roch-
    ester
Florian
The Slave Trade
Newspaper Literati
Prompt Reply
Improvisatori
La Rue
Corilla
Prophesying
French Debates
Sleepers Reproved
Curran
Bourdaloue

As a compendium, *The Percy Anecdotes* calls to mind the encyclopedia, the modern form of which, as Wikipedia reminds us, developed as recently as the eighteenth century—though its antecedents go back at least to Pliny the Elder's *Natural History* (first century CE) and include Cassiodorus's *Institutiones* (560 CE), Patriarch Photius's *Bibliotheca* (9th century), and, most spectacularly, the gigantic encyclopedia overseen by the Chinese Emperor Yongle and completed in 1408, which consisted of 11,000 volumes and 370 million Chinese characters.

Since I have mentioned it, here is the anecdote about William Prynne:

When the famous Prynn underwent the last horrid punishment inflicted on him by the star chamber, for 'writing and publishing certain seditious, schismatical, and libellous books against the hierarchy,' his speech on the scaffold, full of strong exhortations to the people to stand by their liberties, civil as well as religious, was interrupted by loud shouts of applause. The numerous sounds reaching the ear of Archbishop Laud, who was then sitting in the star chamber, he felt so provoked, that he instantly moved the court, that Prynn might be gagged, and a further sentence passed on him. Base and cruel as his colleagues were, however, they recoiled from so monstrous a proposition, and Prynn was suffered to conclude his speech, which he did in these memorable words:— 'Alas, poor England! what will become of thee, if thou look not sooner into thine own privileges, and maintainest not thine own lawful liberty! Christian people, I beseech you all stand firm, and be zealous for the cause of God and his true religion, to the shedding of your dearest blood otherwise you will bring yourselves and all your posterity into perpetual bondage and misery.'

Easy to see how, in this case, as in many others, the collection of anecdotes consists of excerpts from other works. I do not know what text this anecdote about William Prynne is taken from, much less if its version of the events it narrates is credible. Sources are not always revealed in these books, indeed rarely are. Contemporary customs and laws concerning intellectual property and the rights of authors do not apply. Transcription errors are abundant.

There are dozens of books of anecdotes unread in the better libraries. Take Kazlitt Arvine's *Cyclopaedia of Anecdotes of Literature and the Fine Arts*, for example, one of the big nineteenth-century collections that might be confused with an encyclopedia. I spent time with it one afternoon, reading a chapter called "Amusements of the Learned." This has a paragraph with a famous anecdote about Shelley's fascination with paper boats: "Shelley took great pleasure in making paper boats and floating them on the water." He'd fold up his correspondence, "letters of little value" at first but eventually even the "most precious contributions of the most esteemed correspondents." I found the story of Petavius nearby: "When Petavius was employed in his *Dogmata Theologica*, a work of extensive erudition, the great recreation of the learned father was, at the end of every second hour, to twirl his chair for five minutes." It is much as with the collecting of anecdotes, this twirling of the chair, but beware, dear reader, are you certain that our contemporary organization of knowledge makes more sense? Here are the categories for the history of writing listed in the *Cyclopaedia*: "Age, Old, And Literary Pursuits," "Anachronisms," "Antiquities and Relics, Literary," "Habits in Composing and Correcting," "Patronage and Benefactions," "Poets and Their Booksellers," "Egotism, Vanity, and Ambition," "Poverty and Various Misfortunes," "Compliments, Honors, and Popularity," "Benevolence and Sympathy," "Various Excellences," "Eccentricities, Idiosyncrasies, and Caprices," "Collisions and Controversies," "Youthful Love, Domestic Life, &c.," "Deaf, Dumb, and Blind Poets," "Amusing and Mirthful Details," "Sarcasms, Puns, and Jeux D'Esprits," "Origin and Facts of Noted Poems," "Affecting Incidents," "Traits of Character," "Defects, Weaknesses, &c.," "Aptness and Ingenuity," "Vicious Habits," "Facetious and

Humorous." And so on and so on right up through the anecdotes about printing and printing errors, ending with "Wives of Literary Men and Artists," "Women, Literary," and "Words and Phrases."

The literary anecdote promotes the cult of the author as a person of special interest, but often the anecdotes that get collected also work to puncture our sense of the writer's importance, glorying in the trivial or depicting the writer as eccentric. The anecdotalist loves to catch the writer out, to show the famous author distracted or impractical, though there is hero-worship in them too. In *The New Oxford Book of Literary Anecdotes*, we read about Ralegh on his way to the gallows stopping to offer his nightcap to an old bald man, and about Thomas More showing the naked bodies of his daughters to a potential suitor. We read about the wounded Sir Philip Sidney passing his flask of water to a wounded foot soldier. We learn that young Shakespeare declaimed as he slaughtered cattle, and that John Donne, away on business in France, had a vision of his wife in England carrying their dead child. There's Milton flogged at Cambridge for a frolic, Sir Thomas Urquhart laughing himself to death, James Harrington in the Tower of London hallucinating his sweat as bees and flies. There's Sir Charles Sedley stark naked discoursing to a crowd from his balcony, washing his prick in wine and drinking the King's health. There's Swift munching on gingerbread after abusing a pregnant woman, Jefferson explaining that *The Declaration of Independence* was quickly signed because the meeting took place near a stable loud with flies. We read that Hazlitt was afraid of girls and Burns liked bawdy verses and Keats wrote doggerel in the margins of notes he took during lectures. We read about Blake describing a fairy's

funeral and about Mary Wollstonecraft's unsuccessful
effort to drown herself, about Emily Brontë being bit
by a snake and cauterizing the wound with a red-hot
poker. We discover that Burton's *Anatomy of Melancholy* was a favorite book of Melville's, which makes
a lot of sense now that I think about it, and we're
disappointed to hear that Margaret Fuller imagined
that she was the smartest person in America. We *can*
imagine Oscar Wilde drinking Whitman's elderberry
wine and Herbert Spencer inserting earplugs before
heading in for dinner, Mark Twain singing "Nobody
Knows the Trouble I Got, Nobody Knows but Jesus,"
and Swinburne dancing on hats. That Willa Cather
slept on her feet might explain a thing or two, as also
Frieda Lawrence breaking a plate over her husband's
head. Ditto for Evelyn Waugh eating three bananas
imported at great expense while his children watched
without being offered a taste. We see Hopkins fascinated by bubbles trapped in ice. In *The Mammoth
Book of Literary Anecdotes*, we learn that Wordsworth
had ugly legs and walked like an insect. We find
Wordsworth together with Coleridge, both of them
unable to remove a horse's bridle subsequently easily
removed by a young female farmhand. We overhear
Coleridge talking to a button and Henry James (riding
with Edith Wharton) trying in the inimitable syntax
of his prose to ask for directions. Both books are
a hodgepodge and make for light reading. There's
nothing wrong with that.

There are books of anecdotes with quasi-canonical status. I mention a few below, but for now I'll
single out Joseph Spence's *Anecdotes, Observations, and
Characters, of Books and Men*, which is still useful to
students of Augustan literature and culture. Perhaps
partly because publishing anecdotes and attributed

remarks by living persons can be risky business, it was not published until 1820, long after Spence's death in 1768. Spence was the author of occasional verse, but he is better known today as a critic and biographer. Apart from what is usually referred to as *Spence's Anecdotes*, he is probably best known for *Crito, or A Dialogue on Beauty* (1752), published under the pseudonym Sir Harry Beaumont. Spence's editor, Samuel Weller Springer, describes Spence's book of anecdotes as close in spirit to the French *Ana*; his book reads like a collection of notes rather than a structured narrative. (Horace Walpole's roughly contemporaneous *Walpoliana*, edited by John Pinkerton, is another important example of the genre.) Anecdotes and "observations" and sayings are attributed to the parties responsible for them, to Alexander Pope and several others.

Pope's sayings and opinions are recorded without bothering to identify their occasion or setting, and the book also records some of Pope's judgments concerning poets and poems. We learn that Pope did not care for Gower's poetry, for instance, and that he found Crashaw to be a "worse sort of Cowley" and Herbert "lower than Cowley." Pope's opinions about architecture and gardens are also on view. We overhear Pope saying that "Perhaps we flatter ourselves when we think we can do much good: it might be as well, if we can just amuse and keep out of harm's way." Then there's this, which surprised me when I found it: "The things that I have written fastest, have always pleased the most. . . . *The Rape of the Lock* was written fast. . . . I wrote most of the *Iliad* fast; a great deal of it on journeys, from the little pocket Homer on that shelf there; and often forty or fifty verses in a morning in bed." Elsewhere we learn that the poet was once attacked by a "wild cow" that "tore off his hat, wounded him in the throat; beat him down, and trampled over him." We read about Pope busying himself near his death "drawing up arguments for the immortality of the soul": "In a fit of delirium, he rose at near four o'clock, and was found in his library writing; he had said something about generous wines helping it; whereas spirituous liquors served only to mortalize it." We learn that Sir John Suckling played with marked cards *made in France*. That could be trivial, unless you are interested in the opinion of the French among the English. But the story of Lord Halifax objecting to passages in Pope's translation of the *Iliad* as Pope read them to him at his estate makes for eternal wisdom when it comes to writers seeking the patronage of the powerful. Told by a friend that if he read the same (unrevised) passages a few weeks later and described them as having been revised in light of the Lord's wise recommendations the Lord wouldn't know any better, Pope did just that—he left the poem alone and heard Halifax sing its praises. Spence was "a man whose learning was not very great, and whose mind was not very powerful," Dr. Johnson said, adding that "his criticism . . . was commonly just; what he thought, he thought rightly, and his remarks were recommended by coolness and candour." His book of anecdotes contains everything from remarks about Chinese script to a note about Pope's slim regard for John Skelton.

More than anything I wanted this book to go where it wanted to go, to follow the year where it took me. While I have edited it a little, and now have written this introduction, I have tried to be true to that first impulse. The book was intended as a partial record of my time off and of some of my wandering, as also some of my remembering. I don't think

I will spoil any of what follows if I say that, while I read a little about anecdotes during my year off, I am not sure, now that the year is over, that I know much more about them than I did when I began. Louis Brownlow thought of the anecdote as belonging to "a leisurely age when people sat around and had time to talk and inclination to listen." Brownlow was more storyteller than literary critic, and in his *The Anatomy of the Anecdote* he quickly abandons the analysis his title promises and, instead of attempting to define the anecdote, tells one. It concerns a retired politician, Joe Blackburn, who is invited to a burgoo in Kentucky, where he is found far from the crowd, weeping. Asked what the problem is, reminded that he is among friends, Blackburn says "I know that but this crowd's too damned big for an anecdote, and not near big enough for an oration." "As a definition, I am afraid that will have to do," he says.

Then there's this anecdote from Boswell's *Journal of a Tour to the Hebrides* (1785), which I found late in the day but like quite a bit:

> Dr William Robertson came to breakfast. We talked of Ogden on Prayer. Dr Johnson said, "The same arguments which are used against God's hearing prayer, will serve against his rewarding good, and punishing evil. He has resolved, he has declared, in the former case as in the latter." He had last night looked into Lord Hailes's "Remarks on the History of Scotland." Dr Robertson and I said, it was a pity Lord Hailes did not write greater things. His lordship had not then published his "Annals of Scotland." JOHNSON: "I remember I was once on a visit at the house of a lady for whom I had a high

respect. There was a good deal of company in the room. When they were gone, I said to this lady, 'What foolish talking have we had!'—'Yes,' said she, 'but while they talked, you said nothing.' I was struck with the reproof. How much better is the man who does any thing that is innocent, than he who does nothing! Besides, I love anecdotes. I fancy mankind may come, in time, to write all aphoristically, except in narrative; grow weary of preparation, and connection, and illustration, and all those arts by which a big book is made. If a man is to wait till he weaves anecdotes into a system, we may be long in getting them, and get but few, in comparison of what we might get."

Anecdotes are their own justification, as a friend recently reminded me. I'll tell a few of them before it's too late.

One Thing After Another, Or, Quitting Taffety for Cloth

Cubs a game out, Rumsfeld defending his record, stocks open flat. I read the *Drudge Report* for headlines, a story about a Nepalese man who cuts off his hand in tribute to Kali. I start this book, a journal of a year on leave, a book of anecdotes.

In *Conversations with Brecht*, Walter Benjamin remembers the words on the beam in Brecht's study: "Truth is concrete." And he remembers the sign on Brecht's toy donkey beneath the beam: "I, too, must understand it." I thought of this when, in Venice for the Pound conference last July, under a covered walkway near the Rialto Bridge, I saw a thin man sitting Indian-style and furiously dusting the pavement he was able to reach with a seagull's feather. He was there all week, his eyes fixed on this same pavement, contemplating his work with his feather—he might have been painting—with a heavy iron fence behind him, and behind the fence the canal. Diane and I wondered if he had a compulsive disorder, or if he was trying to distinguish himself from the other beggars of the city, the women with their heads down blindly pushing their cups at tourists, others. We had our answer later in the week when we saw that he'd brought plastic figurines to sell and a small suitcase for his gear, a cloth cup for coins. He kept on with his feather. From one point of view—not his own—it was durational performance.

One spring I invited Thom Gunn to read at the university. Watching me light a cigarette as we stopped for a drink one evening, he took the opportunity to lecture me about smoking. I told him I had tried to quit, or that I had quit, many times, and he told me about his own history with smoking. Then he said, as if he'd known me half my life—this was our first meeting—that if I cared about my erection I would quit. Gunn's book *Boss Cupid* (2000) was just out. It features his "songs for Jeffrey Dahmer," brilliantly disturbing songs of "all-consuming" desire, erotic lyrics colored by this ironic allusion to Dahmer's violent history. There was little that was subtle about Gunn, and a lot that was boyish, even at 70. I was impressed by how friendly and forthcoming he was, given that I hadn't previously met him. He told me straightaway that he'd really had only one poet for a friend, August Kleinzahler. He wasn't afraid to tell me which poets he thought good-looking. The only English poet he much wanted to talk about was Ted Hughes, the other bad boy of English poetry in that era. He seemed pleased with my selection of poems by Hughes in an anthology I had just edited, with the exception of one poem from *Birthday Letters*, which he thought a horrible book. He agreed that the best of Hughes can be found in *Gaudete*. He told me that he visited Hughes once in Devon, where he discovered that Hughes kept a stuffed fox in a glass case in his bedroom, a fox with a small rodent in its jaws. I asked him about a little poem that is one of my favorites, "Seesaw." I had assumed for some years that the poem presented an erotic drama and underscored that drama with its off-rhymes. "Oh that's about my brother," he said.

After ten years in his thirty-gallon tank, king of his brackish domain, our Bala shark sinks into a corner, his body in a gruesome twist. He won't be nudging the silver dollar tonight.

Several English poets—and American poets who know something about the poetry scene in England—have told me the same anecdote about J. H. Prynne, the English poet and retired librarian. It is an anecdote that, so far as I know, has yet to be recorded. To understand it, it helps to know that Prynne rejects the cult of personality and whatever it is about poetry that sometimes makes poets out to be gurus. Prynne's correspondent Charles Olson arguably accepted this role late in his life, apparently to Prynne's regret. Other contexts for the anecdote include Prynne's brilliance as a teacher and his reputation as a forward-looking poet, the leader of an English avant-garde. Predictably, these have made him a kind of guru, whether he likes it or not. Prynne's poems are not anecdotal. They don't narrate episodes from his life or experience, or from anybody else's experience, not anyway as experience is typically represented in poetry. Details of Prynne's life are so difficult to locate in his poems that he is reported (in an anecdote told by Robert Potts to readers of the UKPoetry listserv) to delight in the fact that his French translator, the late Bernard Dubourg, said that he did not want to meet him: "If we meet, our friendship would become anecdotal. We must never meet." All of which suggests that there might be some truth in the anecdote that Prynneans tell. A student comes up to Prynne on a street in Cambridge—in most versions Prynne is on his bicycle—and asks him, "What is your wife's name, Mr. Prynne?" "Mrs. Prynne," Prynne replies.

Poets can be gossips, too. When a poet has a reputation like Prynne's, everyone with an anecdote to tell about him will volunteer it sooner or later. The English-Canadian poet-critic Steve McCaffery, who told me of being hosted by Prynne at Gonville and Caius and shown the library where he worked, remembered the sound of Prynne's metal cleats on the pavement outside the window of his room, the poet-librarian on his way to or from his office early in the morning. Thom Gunn remembered that, after he read his poems in Cambridge, Prynne asked him if he thought his poems were "like toast." Years later, Gunn was still not sure what the question meant, though he was sure that Prynne had not meant to flatter him. John Matthias told me that he once joined Prynne and others at high table and decided hours later that Prynne had insulted him in a manner so subtle, so artful, that he had not been able to recognize the insult as an insult. Then there's the anecdote about Tom Pickard ramming Prynne's car at the legendary gathering of poets in Britain's Sparty Lea in 1967, as told by the late, great and often unreliable (as historian) poet Barry MacSweeney, and more recently by Pickard himself. The dispute between the two poets apparently had to do with Prynne telling Pickard that he didn't want the latter's young son around making noise as he tried to read his poems for a recording. Pickard's response (or so the anecdote goes) was to tell Prynne that he read like a "dalek"—and then, later, ramming his car. There are many anecdotes about

Prynne's resourcefulness and generosity, too, about help extended to friends in need: these are perhaps less entertaining and will have to wait another day.

Cubs tied for first, market recovering, Russia claims the North Pole. Brown clouds, made in China, are said to warm the planet. Everything that makes the cow makes me, circulating under my skin. Giuliani is Bush on steroids, Edwards says. A new advertisement from the man in the head-wrap promises another big surprise—we've heard it before. Everyone's favorite flying Bomb-Eater hits the GodBoy while zooming around avoiding nasties—a video game I'm reading about. The first step is far from safe, 60 levels and you're through. It is possible to own Eternity and Beautiful Love, as perfumes.

Just as the reader can't be sure I will be true to the chronology I imagine as this book's chief formal constraint, I can't be sure about the line between anecdotes and other short passages of writing, like jokes. Alan Shapiro likes to tell an anecdote about two celebrated "mainstream" poets, Marvin Bell and Mark Strand. Bell and Strand walk into a Barnes and Noble and head over to the poetry section. Bell looks at the books shelved under B, Strand at the books shelved under S. There's not a book by either poet in the store. "I guess they don't carry my books here," Bell says. "Mine are sold out," says Strand.

As anecdotes circulate in conversation or print, they have the ability to influence communities of poets, becoming part of the lore that surrounds poetic practice and shapes critical judgment. One anecdote influential in this way tells the story of Frank

27

O'Hara and Robert Lowell riding on the ferry to a joint reading on Staten Island. David Lehman has recorded the anecdote, and Daniel Kane and John Wilkinson have discussed it in recent books. As the story goes, O'Hara wrote his famous poem beginning "Lana Turner has collapsed!" on this ferry after scanning a tabloid where he read the news about the actress. At the reading he tried out the poem he'd just composed. The audience responded enthusiastically, which was not a happy development for Lowell, who found this way of making poems all too flip. As Kane notes, the anecdote promotes "speed and improvisation in composition," values important to succeeding generations of New York poets. Indeed, the anecdote makes O'Hara's poetry seem to be *about* spontaneity and contemporaneity, while Lowell comes off as self-important and out of touch with his audience. The stark contrast between the two underwrites a distinction made many times since—as for instance in Ron Silliman's numerous attacks on a "School of Quietude"—between an "academic" or "mainstream" poetry and an "alternative" or "avant-garde" poetry. Even the English poet John Wilkinson, whose poems would seem to have little invested in spontaneity, gets in on the act:

> The point of the anecdote extends well beyond the gratifying one-upmanship of the hip over the self-conscious inheritor of a tradition, of the Irish adopted New Yorker over the Boston Brahmin: through its parade of superficial self-centeredness as a mask for feeling then discovered to be true, O'Hara's poem exposes Lowell's painful negotiations with God in his early verse as a mask for monstrous egotism. Lowell's show

of grappling looks as choreographed as tag-wrestling, a contact sport in which harm is mimed indefatigably; it is so serious that it can't be serious, and when O'Hara starts out "I was trotting along and suddenly," it is Lord Weary (an early Lowell persona) who thereby becomes laughable. Who can resist this jauntiness?

With the way the anecdote is extended in Wilkinson's criticism of Lowell's poetry and person, one might be forgiven for imagining that O'Hara wrote his famous poem *for* Lowell, as an attack on Lowell. As Louis Brownlow notes, "accuracy and anecdotery are enemies."

Cable out all weekend, so I poach wi-fi from a site called Mike's Junk, which I pick up on the front porch. I read about Iranian police arresting 230 people at a "Satanic" rock show and about the Chinese government increasing efforts to regulate Buddha's reincarnation. Barry Bonds doesn't break the home run record. Once he was sleek and many did him seek, but now he's as fat as a sea lion off Fisherman's Wharf. The Fed pumps billions into the system to rebuild trust.

I'm scanning web-based archives for books with "anecdote" in their title. In an online archive of Early Modern writing I find listed *Anekdota eterouiaka, or, The Secret History of the House of the Medicis*. Over at *Eighteenth Century Collections Online* my eyes land on Dorothy Kilner's *Anecdotes of a Boarding School, or, an Antidote to the Vices of Those Useful Seminaries* (1790) and Louis-Pierre Manuel's *Anecdotes Recorded by the Police of Paris, of All the Affairs of gallantry which have occurred in that metropolis for several years past with bio-graphical sketches of the Parisian women of pleasure* (1794). At *Early American Imprints, 1639–1800*, I find *The Macaroni tester, being a select series of original stories—with repartees—comical and original bulls—entertaining anecdotes &c. The whole collected from a great variety of company in the world, and never before published in the world.* This book's author includes a note "to the candid Reader" about the artlessness of anecdotes: "I must take leave to inform you, that the entertainment I present you with, is in a very artless dress, and as I never laugh at Stories I tell myself, I have not set them forth with any study'd Pains or Labour, but have related them as they happen'd, or were expres'd, and such Gentlemen and ladies as deign to read them, are at full Liberty to add to them, or diminish them, as they please. I have only furnish'd them with rude matter in the Memorandum way." The anecdote begins in the palace and moves to the drawing room. That seems to be its history up through the eighteenth century.

"Well, an anecdote needs a frame," says a colleague who's invited me to lunch in Glendale. "You might have a look at a book by Mary Ann Caws, *Reading Frames in Modern Fiction*." I try the mussels.

Boswell's *Life of Johnson* and Trelawny's *Records of Shelley, Byron, and the Author* are little more than books of anecdotes and table talk. Boswell's book is still read, but fewer read Trelawny's, I think, which is too bad. He's a little full of himself, true, as for instance when he describes Byron's decision to swim over to a boat to have lunch and can't resist mentioning that he was the better swimmer and beat Byron to the boat, and then rescued him when Byron began to vomit.

Out back beyond the deck this morning, two pileated woodpeckers appear—they tend to move in pairs—hammering the maple tree. Smaller downy wood-peckers are regular visitors in the garden and like to attack the yucca stalks just beyond my window, but these bigger "woody woodpeckers" come around only once or twice a year, or I see them come around only once or twice a year. Diane and I snap a few photos and I think to look to see what's online about them and come across *The Internet Bird Collection* (IBC) at http://ibc.hbw.com/ibc/phtml/families.phtml, which currently archives videos of 4,636 species of birds, with multiple videos of many species—seven of the pileated woodpecker. The site claims to have video for 47.7% of the bird species in the world and announces its target of 5,000 species rather in the manner that the United Way lists a dollar amount it hopes to reach in volunteer contributions. One comes across an essay now and again about poetry and bird-song, but bird watching is more popular than poetry and poets, obviously. Still, internet archives of poetry pop up nearly every day, but so far as I can tell there is only one website like the IBC for anecdotes, http://www.anecdotage.com, which says that it archives "anecdotes from [Bill] Gates to Yeats." With corpo-rate sponsors including Amazon.com, it allows the public to submit anecdotes, or what the public takes for anecdotes, much as the IBC accepts bird videos. The site displays these anecdotes, most of them very short, in a little window that pops up at the center of a cartoon stage. The text of the anecdote appears inside a speech bubble. The floor of the stage is drawn as a star, its black borders glittering with smaller stars. I punch into the search box "lizards" and get back two anecdotes, one concerning Angelina Jolie, who kept lizards as a child, the other about a komodo dragon at the Los Angeles Zoo that bit the toe of Sharon Stone's husband. I punch in "poets" and find 80 results, many of them anecdotes familiar to me from collections. Anecdotes concerning Samuel Johnson are the most numerous. There is the one from Hibbert's *Personal History of Samuel Johnson* where David Garrick asks Johnson what he takes to be the greatest pleasure in life. The great man answers that this of course is fucking, with drinking a close second. It also notes, no doubt ironically, that Johnson's wife, who liked to drink, gave up on sex. There's one about an old woman dying as she heard Bette Davis recite the poetry of Carl Sandburg and another about Robert Browning telling his audience that he has no idea what *Sordello* means: "Browning himself was once asked by members of the London Poetry Society for an interpretation of a particularly confusing passage. After reading it through twice, Browning frowned, and shrugged his shoulders. 'When I wrote that, God and I knew what it meant,' he declared, 'but now God alone knows!'" I first heard that anecdote from my colleague William Hardesty. The site accepts letters—only a few people have written in. It has a forum, but it's closed. Under a text from Emerson where the great American poet and thinker insists that "Ballads, bons mots, and anecdotes give us better insights into the depths of past centuries than grave and voluminous chronicles," the site announces its "mission" in the following text: "We are currently home to several thousand humorous &/or inspirational items covering everything from acrobats and acronyms to zippers and zoos. . . . We aim to remain 'The World's Widest Web of Celebrity Anecdotes'!" The same page offers a few words about technological advances such as collaborative filtering and open source software, thereby combining techno–romanticism with tabloid values. Its prefatory text notes that the site's contents are "largely limited to biographical incidents" with a few "origin stories" included, and folds in discussion of the history of the word "anecdote," and of the anecdote's form. We read that in classical times the anecdote carried philosophical discourse and later in the Renaissance became equated with "salacious gossip." The site lists and appears to offer a link to Jeremiah Whitaker Newman's *Alphabetical Anecdotes* (*The Lounger's Common-Place Book; or, Alphabetical Anecdotes. Being a Biographic, Literary, Political and Satirical Vade-Mecum*) and Isaac D'Israeli's *A Dissertation on Anecdotes*, though the links take us to Amazon.com, which does not sell these books. The editors of the site are also politically correct, noting that readers will find its contents "deficient in anecdotes pertaining to women," which we are assured reflects an "historical rather than editorial bias."

Anecdotage.com prompts me to do something I've been meaning to do since I started this writing—look at the *Eighteenth Century Collections Online* edition of Isaac D'Israeli's *A Dissertation on Anecdotes*, which is often mentioned as the most famous study of the anecdote. It was published in 1793, in the anecdote's golden age. Another D'Israeli title is *Curiosities of Literature* (1791), which is, in part, a book of anecdotes. D'Israeli is at pains to defend his interest in anecdotes, even as he admits that the enterprise of gathering anecdotes is pedestrian: "It is, therefore, not probable, that a man of genius will condescend to arrange anecdotes." D'Israeli defends the anecdote against the charge that it counts among the "luxuries of literature." "It is not just to consider anecdotes merely as a source of entertainment, because they amuse; if it shall be found that they serve also the purposes of utility, they will deserve to be classed higher in the scale of study than hitherto they have been." Anecdotes are not only "little unconnected stories" easily forgotten, he insists. In the right author's hands, even the most apparently trivial of anecdotes become significant: "such anecdotes would appear trivial in the hands of a mere antiquary; but they become important when touched by a philosophical historian." It is not to the transformative power of *style* that D'Israeli appeals, to literary craftsmanship, in the way that Luc Sante, Fénéon's translator, marvels at the "virtuosic selection and ordering of words for nuance, rhythm, and maximum impact" in Fénéon's *faits divers*. What is valuable about the anecdote for D'Israeli is its insight. He is convinced that "the history of manners has become the prime object of the researches of philosophers"—which is good news for the anecdote, since, in his view, the anecdote belongs to memoir rather than to history, to the person rather than the event: "In histories there is majesty; in memoirs, there is a familiarity." Here, "history" must mean chronicle, as "philosophy" must mean psychology and the study of character. "A well-chosen anecdote frequently reveals a character, more happily than an elaborate delineation; as a glance of lightning will sometimes discover what had escaped us in the full light." D'Israeli then offers a long list of the virtues of books of anecdotes. What he can't bear is anything that counts as light reading—the book of anecdotes is better for you than the romance is—so it is not surprising that he concludes his dissertation by attacking collectors of "frivolous" anecdotes, following Samuel Johnson's lead in this regard and using Johnson himself as an example of someone about whom too many frivolous anecdotes have been recorded. It is only frivolous, he says, to note that Dr. Johnson cut his nails to the quick. But what is frivolous for one person is consequential for the next. So Descartes was fastidious about his wigs—I want to know it. And also that the great philosopher "wore green taffety in France" but quit taffety for cloth in Holland.

Cubs take the first game from the Brewers with the Cards on their tail. News happens, we can't help it; it keeps us from thinking too much about what just happened. More about the Restless Leg Syndrome Moonlight Walk September 23rd, thank you. Keith Richards is not an old fart, he's drunk on stage: how would *you* play "Brown Sugar"? Castro, supposedly on his deathbed writing editorials, picks Obama and Clinton for a presidential ticket. 160 illegals are swept up at an Ohio chicken factory; Leona Helmsley wills 12 million to her dog, Trouble. Musharraf promises to give up his job as army chief, stay on as president. A Malawi official visits London to ask questions about Madonna, who wants to adopt in Africa. Our President says more blessed days are ahead. Richard Jewell, the falsely accused Olympic bomber, dies; Bo Diddley suffers a heart attack. US releases Iranian hostages in Iraq; Madrone and Goldman take a billion dollar stake in Goldman Hyatt. SAT scores dip slightly. Monster beefs up security after breach. Early ovarian surgery is linked to dementia; there's no proof the astronauts were drunk. Spector jury weighs murder charge; Letterman to appear on *Oprah*. Pressure grows on senator in bathroom scandal; Sarkozy telegraphs US plans for Iran. I read "I die of thirst beside the fountain" while wiggling toes. Smuggled turtle eggs are seized in Mexico; thief without duds helps steal suds. Storm debris in water; strip or be bombed; pranksters wrap Karl Rove's car. Chileans take to the streets; the Irish climate warms at twice the global rate. Three men noodle for catfish, which means catching them with one's hands—"stumping" in Nebraska. YouTube is MeTube; MeTube is YouTube. We want a self that never dies, but we're transient. Movie crew blows up hospital for *Batman* sequel.

Daybook

Cubs off for the day; talk of recession follows talk of housing slump. Gonzales quits. A white bag of finch food hanging out back blows in the wind. One can't be bewildered forever; eventually you're just a clod of unknowing. Books and CDs pile up as my eyesight and hearing fade—only work can make us happy? The people rage and the heathen imagine a vain thing? It is yourself that is the source of this disgust, though its objects are not of your making. Michael Vick, gone to the dogs, finds Jesus. War criminals run the government. Love endures, incapacitating us. Alice Notley's book about dead women, *Alma*, is oversized, awkward to pick up and hold, impossible to read.

Out back in the next yard, beyond the overgrown honeysuckle and grape vines that form a natural barrier between yards, three men are working on a house. I hear their voices, their singing, the noise of saws and hammers. Singing and building: it's not the end time yet, whatever the characters in *John from Cincinnati* are saying. But I feel as if I've aged twenty years since 9/11. I feel it two inches south of my gut, where my liver must be. It's all been done; nobody cares. Poetry can't escape the fact that the average American spends seven minutes a day reading (it says right here, true or not); it can't escape the broader malaise. Kenneth Goldsmith says that what defines our moment is *knowing* that it has all been done in poetry, in writing and art—sad thought. All that's left, he says, is pouring old stuff into new containers, moving it around, which describes what he did in *Day*, a book that consists of the entirety of one issue of *The New York Times* retyped and typeset as a book. Or so I'm told—who would read it? Who has read it? Has Goldsmith himself read it? He read it as he typed it. But there's building as near as next door, even if it is out of sight. "What are they building in there?" They're not building a new house but adding to an old one. The squirrels are in a frenzy.

If "all writing is pigshit," as Artaud wrote, it will soon be digitized pigshit. Last year was the "poetry MLA," as some called it, under Marjorie Perloff's watch as president of the organization, and though I was there interviewing candidates for jobs I gave all of the panels a pass. It is futile to pretend that the MLA cares about poetry. The MLA cares about the careers of members of the MLA.

Bernadette Mayer is one of a few contemporary poets who can be identified by a first name. The thing about Bernadette is her laugh. It's neither giggle nor guffaw but something more joyous, ribald and ecstatic. Most of all it is nearly continuous: Bernadette will laugh after half the sentences she speaks. There's little that's not direct about her: it's all full frontal. That is like her poems:

> like the Chinese we count 81 thrusts
> then nine more out loud until we both come
>
> I come three times before you do
> and then it seems you're mad and never will

it's only fair for a woman to come more
think of all the times they didn't care

In the third couplet Mayer editorializes about the
neglect women have suffered in the bedroom, and
this, too, is typical of her work; she's not afraid of
statement. Here's another poem miming the imme-
diacy of conversation sprouted with opinion:

New England is awful
The winter's five months long
The sun may come out today but that doesn't
    mean anything
There are Yankees
Men & women who can't talk
They wear dark colors & trudge around, all in
    browns & greys, looking up at the sky & pre-
    tending to predict all the big storms
Or else they nod wisely
Yup, a northeaster
The sky turns yellow all the time
The river's grey
Everything's black or white
Everybody eats beans
Everything freezes . . .

And so on, in simple declarative sentences, mostly
one to a line. A New Yorker in rural New England
as likely to talk about Red Sox catcher Carlton Fisk
as about Hawthorne or Melville, Mayer walks the line
between naïve observation and cosmopolitan archness
to great effect.

When she was teaching a sprint workshop here in Oxford, Ohio, Bernadette wore the same clothes all week, and so much patchouli that I had to keep the windows of my car rolled down for the duration. All week she had a huge STOP BUSH button pinned to her jacket. She must have imagined that wearing it would make a point at a conservative university in a conservative part of Ohio, but that's not how it worked out. She underestimated the apathy of students and locals, and their ability to read her. They must have thought her harmless. She wore a train conductor's hat, Captain Kangaroo's hat, and used a cane, one sign of the stroke she suffered some years ago, the other being a slight hitch in her speech. She told us anecdotes about Naropa, about Fourth of July parties in upstate New York, about her life with her partner Phil Good. As I drove her back to the airport she told me that one of the young men in her workshop, a heavily muscled boy over forty years her junior, had asked her during a private conference to feel his bicep. I knew the student involved, and it made perfect sense to think of him asking her to do that, innocently. Bernadette thought he might have been hitting on her but it wasn't a big deal. She told me that many years ago John Ashbery had come up behind her at a party and pinched her ass. When she turned around, he said, "I'm sorry, I thought you were a man." I was speeding on the access road to the terminal drop-off, doing 45 in a 25 zone, when I saw the flashing lights in the mirror. This was Kentucky, though it wasn't a trooper but an airport cop. Bernadette had the same STOP BUSH button pinned to her jeans jacket. As the cop walked up behind us, I asked her to cover it. She was reluctant to do so, as if this were finally the moment she would make her statement with her button. But I was the one who would have to pay the speeding ticket, and I wasn't eager to indulge her. She covered the button, and I managed to get off with a warning.

Went round to Hopewell Church with our dog, Milo—that's out past the state park where I've been walking him. It's the kind of church in the kind of place that gives me back the world of my mother's people, up north and east of here, outside Lancaster, Ohio. A brick rectangle, 1808, graveyard attached. Some kind of Protestant sect, the gravestones in bad shape, a man with a van parked nearby working on one of the church's windows. Then back to the park, the sky ready to rain, school having started, the park deserted, the dog and I walking alongside the lake where the pleasure boats are docked as I try to think about what it means "to talk to yourself," as if one has a secret and nobody but oneself to tell. I decide that this is how, coming out of that world of my mother's, I will talk to God if I ever feel the need to do that. I guess I'd be talking first of all to some part of myself I imagine as earnest and responsible enough to take the rest of me seriously. So I imagine that this talking to myself, which I seem to be doing anyway, and which I have more time for now that I am on leave and have leisure to think, might be good for me, a way to steady a self I can live with as I move ahead or back into the so-called real world of jobs and publishing and university life. I suppose it's the age-old Protestant "inner voice" I'm talking about, nothing new about that. I guess it's always there, like the hum of consciousness, the experience of ourselves as experiencing, and it's just a matter of deciding to turn the dial to tune in or turn up a particular mode of attention. Surely before I'd have any ability to pray I'd have to cultivate this inward conversation I have so rarely attempted in a sustained way—though a microsecond might suffice. The walks are good for more sustained reflection, and the park, though tradition would have it that the desert is the best place for work on or "care of the self," rather than the forest, which is what the park has to offer, though here it is cultivated, a half-manicured forest. The forest is supposed to be full of spirits. It's supposed to be pagan, a site of excess and violence, a place to lose oneself, compared with the desert, the privations of which force up epiphanies and the transformations that attend them. That's the story anyway. The forest is swirling with life and should carry the self away, which now that I think about it might be better for me. It is certainly not the case that I expect to figure out anything about myself by writing, and neither do I have anything I want or need to confess or profess or announce to the world, to bring into the world in the gesture that is publishing. A daybook might sit on the desk for years. I don't expect revelation or transformation. But being able to talk to myself walking alone in the woods allows me to identify and hold onto, at least for a moment, some idea of "person," some sense of a self, *my* self, acting meaningfully in the world. Foucault might be right to say that "at the root of what we know and what we are, there is not the inner truth of being, but exteriority and accident," which locates the self within a complex and only partly visible or knowable web of contingencies, a web blown across time and space by the winds we know and the winds we don't, attaching itself now and again to the conditions of our being like a spider that finds itself in the corner of your living room. I'm not sure how I got from Foucault to Jonathan Edwards in one sentence. I'd like to think that we have a self distinct from what we are as a physiological being, an inner self, and some form of agency to spin threads of conscience and being, as we can also choose the "threads" we wear, however we find them and whoever has made them in whatever place a long time ago. But it's a muddle for sure, on the path. If I am early enough and walking where others haven't walked today, I will push my face through the thinnest filaments of web-work, which hang from no branch that I can see, as if fallen from the sky, soft and sticky spider work in the middle of the path.

In the digital age you can have the text of Trelawny, or Johnson's *Lives of the Poets*, pretty much wherever you want: just carry it with you on your iPod, on the street or in the woods. We won't take Thoreau along, I promise the dog. One click and there is Shelley screwing the author of *Frankenstein* yards from the grave of her mother, the author of *A Vindication of the Rights of Woman*. Mary Shelley hardly knew her mother, who was lost to puerperal fever when her daughter was less than two weeks old. Another click and there is Rimbaud's mother telling him that intellectual work leads nowhere. These are *biographical* anecdotes, if we must have names, biographical anecdotes about famous writers, and what do they have to do with me? Two hummingbirds flit among the morning glories. The Cubs and Astros in an afternoon game in two hours. Surveillance has come a long way says the FBI.

If I wanted, I could click on a poem like this one, still one of my favorites by Rae Armantrout:

Double

So these are the hills of home. Hazy tiers
nearly subliminal. To see them is to see
double, to hear bad puns delivered with a wink.
An untoward familiarity.

Rising from my sleep, the road is more
and less the road. Around that bend are pale
houses, pairs of junipers. Then to *look*
reveals no more.

When is a road both more and less a road? There are
hints of the language of riddling in this poem, though
no *solving* of the riddle. To *look* reveals no more, but
thinking might: that's the claim the poem wishes to
make. The everyday and the proximate, the hills of
a local landscape whose effects are partly subliminal,
so familiar they have become, are what make vision
difficult. The eyes are covered by routine, after which
there is seeing the world and there is *really* seeing it,
which is seeing double. I like routine as much as the
next guy, believe in the virtue of describing what's in
front of me, but good poems should slow one's seeing
and force reflection on what's seen, like this seeing
double. The poem is not anecdotal, or rather it does
not participate in an anecdotal realism. Reflexivity is
not a part of anecdotal realism, whose conventions are
empiricist, but anecdotal realism does not exhaust the
anecdote and its possibilities. Armantrout's "Double"
doesn't have the kind of overt and intense self-reflexive scrutiny of ordinary language (or of its own language) that many of her other poems feature, but it
explains the need for that kind of scrutiny. When I

talked with Armantrout in Ireland a few years ago, she told me that she was taken—this was her first visit to Ireland—by the fact that so many of its houses are painted in pastels. Why is this, she asked me, as if I knew. She hadn't expected pastels. I was used to seeing the buttery yellow cottages along the road from Shannon to Cork and from Cork to Kinsale and hadn't given the matter a thought.

A tiny growth appears on my eyelid—what to do about it? Diane, a nurse, says it's a bleb, a word I have to look up. Nothing to worry about.

Everything is alive and nothing surprises in the woods, in the clearing as also on the paths. Along the borders of Acton Lake, Milo knows the way, looks back to be sure I'm okay with the presumed direction. The two fishermen I see are father and son, but Milo barely notices them among the scents. The woods are mostly quiet; bigger noise is miles off. It occurs to me that I don't have a single original thought, only what's carved and worn, tended to if also overgrown, like these woods beside this man-made lake. But I might see something I haven't noticed previously. Is that seeing double? Seeing again? Or only seeing? I've watched them along the river and on this lake for years, but I hadn't known the blue heron's call—a squawk, as if the bird is trying to push its liver out its throat. The sugar hut is peeling paint, I see, looking to my left. Brown and red leaves, dying grass. Then the wind gets serious—I should let the pages of this daybook blow into the lake. Crickets and cicadas, oscillating sound. Chirp of the near sparrow, panic of the remote duck.

45

Shooting the Air

Is any of this visible through an amateur telescope? There is no pressure outside the atmosphere, the man on the radio says. What am I writing about? I am writing about what comes to mind as it comes to mind, as I remember it, in the wake of its happening or after its happening in memory. A few things I notice or noticed once, about some poems and poets. There is nothing to see here. This could be the coldest spot in the sky, the man says, and truth-free.

Shadows longer toward Labor Day, green corn gone gold. One sailboat docked. A dragonfly patrols the shore accompanied by the throb of an invisible jet; four ducks, the same blue heron, another bird, possibly a loon for all I know, on the little island closer to shore thanks to the drought. It's a good day for sailing, with a brisk, pushy wind. I needn't associate free association with purpose or care about the purpose of this writing. What do I remember? What do I see? That's the turf of anecdotes? A middle-aged couple on a motorcycle pulls into the parking lot, immediately turns around to leave. Out west at the Burning Man festival a man hangs himself in a tent. It is two hours before anybody thinks to cut him down. A performance, his friends say, we thought it was a performance.

I hadn't noticed until recently this usage: "remains" for the human body after death. I don't know the word I'd supposed was used—cadaver maybe, or corpse, I hadn't thought about it. I hear "remainder" with remains, and I guess the term is comforting for the way it suggests that the rest of the dead person has gone off and left a bag of bones and skin behind. An archeological dig in the 24th century: "Look, human remains!" "Humans, with bad teeth!" A farmer all of his life, my Uncle Howard had, his family had, a small image of a tractor sewn into the corner of the upper lining of his coffin, folk art to remind viewers of his "remains" of what they already knew—farming meant a lot to Howard. The idea of the farmer remained.

Love is a tough business, the woman on NPR says, ending her feature on "attachment aversion." I'd just been thinking about Joseph Beuys and his fat sculptures, and wondering how fit the Germans of his day were compared with the Americans of ours. The Nazis didn't keep statistics concerning body fat, or did they? One thinks of Germans as fit, as ready for the spa, or so the cliché has it. Our contemporary fascism is softer, more comfortable, *fatter.* We get along or we don't, but we eat regardless. As Paul Craig Roberts says, up to a million dead in Iraq hardly gets our attention. We're too fat to get off the couch to impeach Bush. We're too fat to force Cheney out of his hole. We're too fat to do anything about plans to bomb Iran or build a detention center or about a bill passing the House allowing for tribunals to be set up to sniff out domestic terrorists. But we're not too fat to want to be loved—unless we have "attachment aversion."

The baby squirrel falls from a tree in the front yard, down through the sunroof, landing on the passenger's seat of our car, bouncing to the floor. We open the door and there he is—now we have more responsibilities. There's Allison at college, the dog Milo, four cats, a tank full of fish, and now this squirrel. Diane is momentarily tempted to keep it, or says she is, but, praise Allah, it turns out it's illegal for ordinary folk to keep a squirrel for more than two days. That's a law with a history worth knowing: "Keep that squirrel more than two days and we'll think you mean to eat it." (The 1931 edition of *The Joy of Cooking* includes recipes—also for raccoon.) Or maybe it has to do with fear of rabies—I don't have a clue really. Diane feeds it Pedialyte for the night and wonders if she should put it back under the tree in the morning, then reads that this is a bad idea. In the morning it urinates—what we thought a prominent umbilical cord turns out to be a penis. In Seven Mile, there's a woman; Diane drives out there and hears her story. She is waiting for a kidney transplant, but she is doing this work nobody closer wants to do, taking care of lost and damaged baby squirrels. Also raccoons.

We don't have celebrity poets in the United States, nobody who reads to packed stadiums the way Yevtushenko once did in the Soviet Union. But now because somebody at the university in the Russian Studies Center contemplates inviting him to campus and I have been asked about that plan, I'm on the phone with Joshua Kotin of the *Chicago Review,* asking him about Yevtushenko's visit to Chicago last year. He wouldn't answer a single question, Kotin says, not really; he had nothing but anecdotes. He wanted to tell stories about his old girlfriends, like the one who was an acrobat or gymnast. She scaled the Kremlin, Yevtushenko said, to fetch him an icicle, the sweetest icicle he'd ever tasted. An allegory of the triumph of sex over communism—I wonder if he tells the anecdote often. Easy to imagine Americans getting a rise out of such a story—it's hard to forget those Russian gymnasts from the old days, even if they weren't so nimble as the Romanians.

Some days you can feel the train wreck coming before you hear the train. The stock market has the jitters; Zambrano is the Cubs ace but can't find the plate and hasn't won a game since July. But they're in the race for real now. An old guy on a trail at the park belches, full of Labor Day beer the morning after the holiday, looking like he's ready to heave. What they've planned for Iran seems only too obvious, and there's nothing to do about it. A recession is inevitable; the drought is shrinking the lake. Civil disobedience—that's a bender in the woods. Today it's two herons, one flying low above the lake, the other posted on a log ten feet out on the lake. We have to do something and haven't a clue what. If I were teaching this semester, I'd be tempted to ask my students to write, "You must change your life" forty times on the blackboard. My sinuses begin to clog, not fooled by dry wind.

Some people talk to God, some people talk to their animals. Some people talk to their priest and some to their shrink. Some people talk to their friends, some write it all down. Some people talk to one person, some people talk to a room. Some people talk to the camera, some people talk on the air. Some people make their talk into writing, some people make their writing into talk. Some people speak to promise, some people promise to speak up. Some people say what they think, some people think about what they say.

Some people go out on a limb when they talk, some say their word is their bond. Some people stutter, some people practically sing. Some people say that the speaking that is inward is the speaking one must listen to most closely; some people say it's too close to be heard. Some people speak all day; some people speak in a daze. Some people speak to interrupt; others interrupt to speak. It's all talk, they say; they say that all talk breaks off.

Today my colleague cris cheek and his former partner, the Welsh violinist and singer Sianed Jones, performed their *Songs from Navigation* at the university. There was one line in their performance (cris uttered it) that I heard as "We come up out of the sea, walk on the beach for a while, get in the car and drive off." Looking at the little Reality Street book where the work is published with its accompanying CD, I see that the text is represented there as follows:

> ok so ad, er, brief history
>   we, err, come out of y sea
>   and walk on y beach
>   for a while, before going home where
>   we pick up y keys for y car
>   and drive
> here, quietly talking a rotting stray
>   on the lion-fish's back

So much for apprehension. That's the text, except that I can't be sure that those last two lines belong with the others, belong to the same sentence, since they begin a new page. Pages in the little book feature multiple fonts, alongside reproductions of handwritten script and drawings or doodles and scribbles, so that continuity among fonts seems worth noticing. Elsewhere, fonts clearly signal discursive continuity across a page break:

it's a struggle to see because there's no way
it's a struggle to see this space it's kept as
space for conspicuous objects offering anything
other than the out of sight

But perhaps not here. Each page is a "box" or square, a square within a square indicated by a line maybe an eighth of an inch from the book's edge. Fonts and script are continuous and discontinuous through-out the square, often pushed against the edges of the square as if testing them (though unlike one Futurist painting by Severini in the Peggy Guggenheim Collection in Venice there is no effort actually to write, as it were, *on the frame*). It is not one square/page we look at when we open the book, however, but two, the "double-page" spread. After the "open field" poetry of Black Mountain, after the work of Susan Howe and others, after the many varieties of visual and "concrete" poetry that have been published over the last fifty years, there is nothing unusual about this practice, but we still don't know enough about how to *read* work like this, which seems simultaneously to demand the skills of the art critic and the literary critic (add the CD or live performance into the mix and the music critic has her place too). cheek, whose performances are legendary for their improvisatory energy, cut his teeth in Bob Cobbing's workshops. Cobbing and those influenced by him have been known to perform "readings" of puddles and scratches on floor tiles, a practice analogous to free jazz musicians using drawings instead of musical scores as prompts for improvisation. After reading the passage I quote here, cheek improvised a little and added something to the story of the lovers coming up out of the water to walk the beach a bit before driving off: "It occurs to me that this is the story of human evolution."

An email from Eirik Steinhoff in Chicago tells me he's moved to 53rd and Harper, where a friend used to live. I remember—this friend had been let go from the steel mills and was hunting for another job. Meanwhile he was selling pot. He had a red velvet couch, two rooms with shag carpet, and a big TV. A gun in the closet, "in case." I remember asking him if he'd ever fired it. "On New Year's Eve," he said, "New Year's Eve. Stay away from the windows on New Year's Eve."

From Chicago to Buffalo

Lots of poets came through Chicago while I was in graduate school—I remember most of them but have few anecdotes, as I watched most of them from a distance. It was Alan Shapiro who told me to look out for J. V. Cunningham's cigarette, the way he was able to keep his ash intact even as his cigarette burnt down to the filter, an inch or more of ash hanging, ready to be flicked off but refusing to fall. The story proved true at Cunningham's reading in Chicago. He was old, and he was not at that point accustomed to giving readings. A steady hand: that is evident in the poems too, as also the stoic view of life as slow burn. One might imagine a martini with the cigarette to have a sense of the poems. He prefaced each poem by announcing its meter: "This is a poem in iambic trimeter." I don't think I said a word to him. He was the closest thing I'd seen to Yvor Winters, whose work I knew must be important because I was reading and hearing about it from Bob von Hallberg in my first graduate seminar. There were a lot of former students of Winters, and poets who had learned from Winters, around Chicago in those days, thanks to Bob's influence. Besides Cunningham, there was Shapiro himself, Ken Fields, Robert Pinsky, Turner Cassity, Robert Hass, and John Matthias, all of them except Shapiro one-time students of Winters. Not all of these poets remained "Wintersian" poets, though

some of them did. Donald Davie also came to town—
he had a lot of time for Winters' poetry and criticism and took over for him at Stanford—and I drove
north to other universities in the city to hear Timothy
Steele and James McMichael read, poets more or less
of that crowd. I brought Fields and Tim Dekin to
read under the auspices of the *Chicago Review* and
was feeling obnoxious and self-satisfied enough to ask
the twelve people in the audience to sit through my
diatribe about the size of the audience for poetry at
the University of Chicago. Of all these poets, it was
Cunningham who seemed bigger than life, though his
poems are very small, epigrams mostly:

> And what is love? Misunderstanding, pain,
> Delusion, or retreat? It is in truth
> Like an old brandy after a long rain,
> Distinguished, and familiar, and aloof.

A cigar might go well with this brandy, for a poet
rhyming "truth" with "aloof." The poem has the
air of the 1940s men's club, with well-worn leather
furniture—I know nothing about Cunningham's
lifestyle. Of the epigram and the plain style as Cunningham used it, Winters said the following: "Cunningham's style is in no sense the personal style of
someone else, nor is it an archaic style. . . . The plain
style . . . is unmannered; it is free of the eccentricities
of the time, the place, and the man: it is perennially
useful." Maybe so, though I am not sure that all of
the poems are unmannered:

> Dark thoughts are my companions. I have wined
> With lewdness and with crudeness, and I find
> Love is my enemy, dispassionate hate

Is my redemption though it come too late—
Though I come to it with a broken head
In the cat-house of the disheveled dead.

Those last lines seem mannered enough, perhaps
even faintly Eliotic. Reading the poem again now,
I am left to wonder how consciously Cunningham worked his trick with the cigarette. His poems
should be read for their principle of exclusion, which
is how Cunningham understood rhyme. Here's the
last stanza of "Coffee," a poem about solitude as it
relates to freedom, and about privacy within a marriage: "Insight flows in my pen. / I know not fear nor
haste. / Time is my own again. / I waste it for the
waste." You can't argue with that.

Red ochre is the color of the outback and eucalyp-
tus green is the color of the Australian bush, as the
leaders have lunch at Guillaume in Bennelong next to
the Opera House, the day after Bin Laden or his body
double, beard touched up by Just for Men, releases his
annual 9/11 video. On the menu: barramundi with
endives, mushrooms, pearl of vegetables, yabbies, scal-
lops and a light ginger emulsion, followed by roasted
saddle of lamb with field mushrooms, kipfler pota-
toes, confit of tomato and thyme jus and a selection
of Australian fruit and cheese. Wines from regional
Australia including 2004 Mount Pleasant Maurice
O'Shea and 2004 Tyrells Vat 47 from the Hunter
Valley. Later they'll have dinner inside the Opera
House. The Tracey Wan Quartet will perform as they
dine on a feast of rolled yellowfin tuna, Western Australian yabbies and Sterling caviar, and Grainge Angus
Black Label Wagyu Beef striploin on a bed of rata-
touille and salsa verde. Meanwhile, Bee Colony Col-

lapse Disorder, the latest research finds, appears to be produced by a virus. The experimental technique used to isolate the virus may yet turn out to have applications for human diseases. Instead of trying to culture bacteria, which is often a lengthy process, researchers grind up the bees and rapidly sift through the genetic material in search of a suspicious microorganism. At the protest in Sydney, there is one letter per naked cheek, two per naked bum, spelling out NO BOMBS. There's a cross and a peace sign on bum number two, the left cheek for Jesus and the right cheek for peace.

Sixteen hours in the car to Buffalo to talk to a class about my book *Fishing by Obstinate Isles*, with its simple thesis about the effects of American power on the interface of British and American poetry. On the way I drive by a car with words stenciled on its trunk: "Cars are a sign Jesus is coming." Near Ashtabula I pull off the highway to check out the little town and state park at Geneva-on-the-Lake. At a stoplight in town, its brick storefronts suggesting the forties or fifties, buildings much like those I remember from visits to my grandparents in Parma, Ohio, I photograph a sign for "Psychic Monday" next to an Italian-American restaurant. Then into the state park a mile beyond town. The odd feeling that the way the man ahead of me in his little Toyota is driving and looking around means he is cruising for sex in the mostly deserted park, followed by the thought that others might think I am doing the same. Dozens of boats in the marina off Lake Erie, waves whipped up by fall coming in, winter in mind. The back of one boat reads, "Get some." On the road again, without Willie Nelson, a man on the radio talking about sovereign wealth funds, China's good for 200 billion this year alone.

Word that the city of Lorain is to be emptied in a civil emergency, the nature of which is not disclosed—probably a train derailment with spilled chemicals. Then more talk of tiger-bone wine as I enter the wine country across the New York line and take an exit for fast food in a little town with a Welch Grape Juice factory. Twilight and bigger wind as I drive into Buffalo via Lackawanna, past industrial parks, catching sight of the red lights on a row of wind turbines to my left at land's edge, off the gunmetal lake. It's the postindustrial sublime, scenic. The highway is unfamiliar as it shoves me down a raised ramp into the city. Not a place to break down! The next day I ask a few graduate students and faculty what it is that the people of Buffalo produce in these factories, and they don't know. Someone says they're shuttered. "It's the Saint Lawrence Seaway that killed Buffalo," Steve McCaffery says, remembering the grain that used to be moved through the city when the Erie Canal and the Falls and the electricity it generates meant something. He and his partner Karen Mac Cormack are quick to point out that one recent survey has it that there are more cultural events in Buffalo than anywhere else in the country outside of New York and Los Angeles. Hard to imagine how that can be so—per capita perhaps, the city shrunk to 300,000. But I find that I like Buffalo, a crucial home for the avant-garde in American poetry, from Olson to Creeley to Bernstein to McCaffery. Anyway I like the old robber baron mansions along Delaware Avenue, one of them now housing the Red Cross and others the home of other worthy institutions. It's something to do with the relics of old money, as if old money is more harmless, something about a certain lack of pretension in the city. It's a town with good bookstores, even if the percentage of residents with a college education is below that of New York City. I check into the hotel, ride the elevator up with a blind couple and their two dogs: "Is this the fifth floor?" they ask me. "No, it's the second," I say. But it turns out to be the fifth after all, I'm the one who is confused, and they turn up a minute later as the elevator door opens while I'm waiting to go down. A phone call and it's over to Steve and Karen's for a drink and a tour of his impressive library, leather-bound first editions of Donne's *Sermons* and Ben Jonson's *Volpone*. The poetics seminar the next day, and dinner at Buffalo's finest French restaurant and a reception—it's great to see young graduate students excited by the poetry of Basil Bunting, Lynette Roberts, Mina Loy, others. Discussion of Charles Abbott with several students: he's the man who saw to it that Buffalo collected modern poetry and set in motion the good things that have happened there since. Karen and Steve tell anecdotes about their trip to South Africa—its beauty and its poverty, its protected baboons stealing food, its six-year-old thieves on the street. Nothing like that in Buffalo, I hear myself thinking, not yet.

Some avant-garde poets are not only scholarly but collectors, book collectors—McCaffery and Alan Halsey are among the poets I have in mind. Of course lots of poets have loads of books. I am talking about poets who have something approaching a love for books, aficionados. McCaffery is an aficionado and Halsey might be too—I don't know him well enough to know—though I know that he has been and still is a bookseller. One way the love of the book as object or curio shows up in McCaffery's and Halsey's work is as self-reflexive playfulness about the history of letters

and lettering, of print, typefaces and fonts. This in itself
is not so rare among so-called postmodern writers.
But in the case of these two, who are good friends,
the tropes and puns and playfulness that respond to
the book as material object are often accompanied by
allusions to the nooks and crannies of literary history,
by jokes about writers and writing. This demonstrates
a fondness that I share—though I am no collector
of books—for anecdotes. The textuality of literary
history as grounded in the imperfections of print is
another concern. In Halsey's case, I am thinking of
prose books such as *The Text of Shelley's Death* and
A Robin Hood Book, but there is also the poetry (text
lineated as such) of "Eleatic Electric," with its allusion to Greek philosophy, and some of *Wittgenstein's
Devil*. The comedy of script, the turning of phrases,
the delight in near-homophones and rhyming, from
typo to topos—the work is descended from Laurence
Sterne. *Dante's Barber Shop (De Vulgari Eloquentia)* is
one of my favorite Halsey books and a sadly neglected
example of the possibilities of book art. Each of its
pages is framed by a collage of black and white photographs, including photographs of what apparently
is a real Dante's Barber Shop, its name too much
for Halsey to resist. The text of the book begins as
follows, arranged in newsprint columns that I won't
reproduce here:

> To say he 'tows the line of zero longitude' scarcely
> needs correction or apology even if we believe
> as I sometimes don't the linguistics textbook that
> ordinary language is good. What's so ordinary
> about ordinary language that it has to be good
> or bad? You have to tow the line somewhere
> even Greenwich even if the millennial doom of

our youth has been so facetiously replaced by the millennium dome to prove puns which are sometimes typos in disguise still matter. Okay topos. Stop O. If ordinary language was good enough for Coleridge it's good enough for me but often it wasn't and I like the way his conversation poems are for only one voice. Words come in ones and twos and then another one tows the line somewhere else I expect is what he meant and although it's more exacting to cross any line than to find it has been moved to toe it is the dullest option.

An air of confidence, a sense of the endlessness of knowledge and discourse as gathered in books, of the nuances and absurdities and odd corners of old books—all of this characterizes Halsey's prose. And some of the odder folk of the present also appear in it—my colleague Bill Howe turns up in *Dante's Barber Shop*, in an allusion to his as-yet-unpublished and more than slightly obsessive post-Fluxus project "translating" all of Emily Dickinson's poems into gibberish.* Howe is from Texas and wrote a dissertation at Buffalo on the ways that concrete poetry and post-concrete poetry require reading we don't really have enough tools for, which helps us gloss the following lines in Halsey's book: "Or in the Reverend Howe's words 'how do you read?' but if you read for a long time is that different and how much from how you read for a short time? How many translanations can there be of a Dickinson poem and is Texas big enough to hold them?" Bookish but not limiting its

---

* Some of these poems are now available in Howe's book *translations one* (BlazeVOX Books, 2009).

attention to elite culture, *Dante's Barber Shop* pinballs off *The Simpsons*, Monica Lewinsky, Ray Charles, and the department store Marks & Spencer as well as Coleridge and Shelley, Thomas Lovell Beddoes, Wyndham Lewis, Ed Dorn, Tom Raworth, and J. H. Prynne, to list a few names that appear: "Just after Ed Dorn's death the Lone Ranger's." For every reference to Marks & Spencer there's one to the mainstream poetry publisher Faber & Faber. Halsey's cosmopolitanism is a match for W. H. Auden's, and more fun.

There is a similar spirit as also similar bookishness in McCaffery's work, habits of the aesthete who recognizes that his role is as much urban comedian as man of taste. If one subtext of the work of both of these writers who have collected and valued books is the unreliability or fallibility of books as man-made objects, what else is one to do with books in this culture, apart from laughing about them? Before I left Buffalo, McCaffery gave me a copy of his latest, *Crime Scenes*, prose poems written as he watched a crime show on television—perhaps the show even has that name. "Best Taco I ever had. Is that a fact or a Fiero?" it begins. Before long he's on to Johnson's *Dictionary* and Keats' *Endymion*, to John Ruskin and *Kabbalah and Criticism*. There are other dimensions to McCaffery's work, and Halsey's, beyond this more or less comical display of knowledge, something other than playing tiddly-winks with canonical and pop culture figures and titles. In McCaffery's case his interest in pataphysics goes back to his earliest days in sound poetry, and one should look out for philosophy and pseudo-philosophy in Halsey's discourse. In McCaffery's critical prose, a pataphysical poetics is discussed under the rubric of the "protosemantic," and some of its first and most important grafts are from Julia Kristeva's *Revolution in Poetic Language* and Georges Bataille's concept of "expenditure." McCaffery's work explores "a multiplicity of forces which, when brought to bear on texts (or released in them), unleash a combinatory fecundity that includes those semantic jumps that manifest within letter shifts and verbal recombinations, and the presyntactic violations determining a word's position." I quote from his recent essay not on his own poetry but on John Cage's mesostics and "transcoherence," a neologism McCaffery says means "variant coherence"—the coherence produced by Cage's writing through of Joyce's *Finnegans Wake*, of an "interventional poetics destined to disclose a hidden coherence by eradicating a manifest coherence." Scrape away the pattern to find the pattern within.

On the way back from Buffalo I stop to see my mother and father. There's a table full of pills in their living room, two plastic containers, one for each parent, marked with the days of the week and the times of the day specific pills are to be taken, little boxes within a bigger box, each little box containing three or four pills. Nodding off regularly but only for a few seconds at a time, my mother takes part in the conversation, though my father worries that her dementia is getting worse. She's taken to picking at her clothes, to getting up and pacing nervously. She's taken to washing one sock at a time in the washing machine. Nothing much on the drive back except the pleasure of hearing on the radio the Angel Band, new to me, playing "Boots of Guadalupe," a country song about a pair of $2,000 boots the singer falls in love with when she sees them in the window of a

New Mexico shop. The boots feature an image of the Virgin of Guadalupe. If there really is a Virgin of Guadalupe, it's time she headed north.

Being and Time

An NPR story about lost and found services in big
cities features an interview with the man who works
at Customer Service in Grand Central Terminal,
New York. Thousands of items are left on the trains
every year, he says, picked up by other passengers and
turned in. It all gets put in a database, and thanks to
the efforts of a staff that works to find the owners of
the lost stuff, 80% of it is recovered. Cellphones and
umbrellas lead the list, and once—$17,000 in a back-
pack. There is no resisting the opportunity to name
the odder deposits: glass eyeballs and artificial legs, a
basset hound. He tells an anecdote about an old lady
who turned up once with the perfect description of
a lost vase. She knew the number of the car in the
train where the vase had been lost. They locate the
vase, she leaves with it, but she can't help herself so
comes back five minutes later to tell her story. Her
late husband had been a bad man, unfaithful to her;
many a night he didn't sleep at home. His excuse was
always the same: he fell asleep on the train. He went
past his stop. So the woman thought she would do
her husband one last favor and leave his ashes in this
vase on that same train—for three weeks. For three
weeks, her plan was, he would go round and round.
Three weeks was probably enough.

Cubs and Brewers tied for first, eleven games remain-
ing. O. J. Simpson back in jail. A run on the North-
ern Rock bank in the UK; the bank is swamped by

its collateral debt obligations (CDOs). The Fed cuts rates in the US, trying to head off this kind of run. Our cat Mina, as grey as Mina Loy's eyes in one photograph, returns from a night at the vet's, having been diagnosed with a fever of unknown origins and dehydration: $350 for the blood work, medicine, and IV. Now she sits on my desk, wanting out. The September light is soft, warm and temporary. The piles of books around me take on a different tint, the iPod and laptop, plastic dinosaurs on the bookshelves, a rubber Gorbachev head. I am reading that Bill Griffifths is gone at 59. I asked him once about "Reekie," his great poem about giving up cigarettes: I don't think he ever managed to quit, not for good anyway. There's a scene in the Tarantino section of *Sin City* where a character sitting in the passenger seat with a hatchet in his forehead (there has been a big fight) lights up and says to the driver something like "You never really do quit." I asked Griffiths about "Reekie":

> There are advantages:
> the clean, sweet sweep of the nasal passages,
> a labyrinthinity of
> the lung overt to air,
> the added sensitivity when you resort to other
> drugs. Is a
> eye-opener.

The better the lungs, the better their absorption? Marijuana? Griffiths wouldn't admit a thing. It occurs to me that his heart attack, if that is what it was, might have owed something to his smoking. Will Rowe in his obituary blames Bill's diet.

In this maudlin moment, images of a few of the poets met across the years push forward: Turner Cassity in his dark olive suit, a thin man with a cigar and crew cut. A Southern dandy, or so I thought at 23. I'm younger than that when I meet Raymond Carver at a party in Akron at Elton Glaser's house. He's on the wagon, and he's wondering who's brought the pot. There's Robert Duncan after a reading in Chicago two or three years later; he'd waved his arms conducting himself as he read in his black cape, stopping once to apologize for his French. I see him sitting on the couch in Bob von Hallberg's living room, Wayne Booth walking over to introduce himself, rhetoric paying homage to poetry. But Duncan is holding court with students and won't stand to shake Booth's hand. There's Tess Gallagher in the corner of the room at the Renaissance Society in Chicago later that year—or it was another year—*singing* a poem, the room suddenly twice as vast but also twice as intimate to receive this tiny, beautiful song. There's John Wieners in the hallway of an Orono dorm, the morning after his reading at the conference on the 1960s, a reading where he seemed battered by spotlights and lost in front of hundreds of academics sitting in the dark. I felt that his fame had been abused; he seemed in a fog of medication and barely capable of uttering the lines he managed. But in the hallway the next morning he is lucid, says he's happy to be among a community of poets and scholars. There's Allen Ginsberg tiny with a big smile, bug-eyed on the sidewalk to hear I am writing about Basil Bunting, and just a little later there's Armand Schwerner killing the audience with a second melody line hummed over the top of his reed, not two hours after he'd told me about his cancer. They all disappear, in these sentences.

The sawbuck is sawdust, the Canadian and American dollar even-steven, \$1.40 for the Euro. Ask a question, wait for the taser. Watch the senator watching you. Watch the crowd watching you. Wait for the cameras and howl.

One day some years ago Tom Raworth forwarded me email spam he had received and joked, "Who needs Clark Coolidge now?" He must have been thinking about the abstract soundscapes and word collocations of Coolidge's poetry, which I know him to admire. There was a period several years ago when the spam that eluded filters had surprising phrases in it—never the wild echoes and rhythms of Coolidge in books like *On the Nameways*, though I took Raworth's point—which led a few poets to wonder if there wasn't something that might be done with it to *make* poems. That's not the case with today's spam, the tedium of which crushes one's spirit. Or at least it's the case less often:

> cheerinesses cheering cheeringly his proud palaces remain, And his sad consort beats her breast in vain.His troops in forty ships Podarces led, Iphiclus' son, and brother to the

> http://proxcomsolutions.com

> dead Nor he unworthy to command the hostYet still they mourn'd their ancient leader lost.The men who Glaphyra's fair soil partake,Where hills incircle Boebe's lowly lake,Where Phaere hears

> the neighbouring waters fall, Or proud Iolcus
> lifts her airy wall, In ten black ships

This message shows up in my inbox, and I think I recognize part of it. To confirm my suspicion I punch "his proud palaces remain" into Google. The search engine turns up a link to Alexander Pope's translation of the *Iliad*, as scanned by Google and put online, an edition owned by Harvard University. It's the 1853 two-volume Ingram, Cooke, & Co. edition, acquired by the library in 1874, featuring John Flaxman's "designs" as well as other engravings and notes and a long, learned introduction by The Rev. Theodore Alois Buckley, M.A., who writes that Pope's translation should be read "rather as an elegant paraphrase, than a translation." "Pope was not a Grecian," Buckley says. "There are, to be sure," he continues, "certain conventional anecdotes, which prove that Pope consulted various friends, whose classical attainments were sounder than his own, during the undertaking; but it is probable that these examinations were the result rather of the contradictory versions already existing, than of a desire to make a perfect transcript of the original."

Reverend Buckley turns out to be quite the stylist. He begins his introduction with a finely turned aphorism suggesting that "Scepticism is as much the result of knowledge, as knowledge is of skepticism," admonishing his readers not to forget "the very gradual character of our education," or the need to "continually forget, and emancipate ourselves from, knowledge previously acquired," which seems like good, practical advice, and which also gives us license to reject his views of translation and poetry. As for Pope himself, his preface to the translation remains an important document in the history of literary criticism for its defense of the "wild paradise" of Homer over and against Virgil's poetry, for its stated belief that while "Exact disposition, just thought, correct elocution, [and] polished numbers" can be found in many poems, the "poetic fire" or "vivida vis animi" is found in very few. Pope argues exactly the opposite of what I expect from Pope. I expect him to prefer Virgil to Homer because Virgil's poetry is altogether cooked beside Homer's raw narrative. But he doesn't: "Homer is universally allowed to have had the greatest invention of any writer whatever," he begins, insisting that it is invention that matters most in writing. Pope's line about what one wants from poetry comes to me, and I wonder how it fits here: "What oft was thought, but ne'er so well expressed." He continues: "The utmost stretch of human study, learning, and industry, which masters everything besides, can never attain to this [to Homer's genius for 'invention']. It furnishes art with her materials." My former colleague, the Heidegger scholar Charles Spinosa, used to make fun of the way that literature scholars claim they "make arguments." "Arguments?" he'd say. "Lawyers make arguments. As for philosophers—the good ones imagine worlds." Spinosa might have been on Pope's side, as also the Rev. Buckley's, in acknowledging the ways in which poetry has more to do with creation than culture, with culture understood as refinement, as cultivation. That is also why the academy has sometimes wanted little to do with it. But cultivation is also much worked as a metaphor in Pope's essay. Homer's *Iliad* is "a copious nursery, which contains the seeds and first productions of every kind, out of which those who followed him have but selected some particular plants, each according to his fancy, to cultivate and beautify." So it is not really true that Pope admires Homer but not Virgil—he admires both of them. And when Homer is cultivated on spam farms? Spam doesn't have to be made into poetry; it already *is* poetry. As for "cheeringness cheering cheeringly," that apparently comes from an assignment at Yale University (though as I revise this writing, the website now seems to have been encrypted): http://zoo.cs.yale.edu/classes/cs223/2006s/assignments/ps9/scowl80. I couldn't make this up if I tried.

Reading Rae Armantrout's poetry ahead of her visit to Oxford, I am thinking I should write an essay that contrasts her work with Lorine Niedecker's, perhaps also with Tom Raworth's and Ben Friedlander's—poets I admire, all of them practicing forms of sprung syntax, though to different effects. In an interview, Armantrout says, "I confess that my work does sometimes (even often) manifest the tendency to write about writing or think about thinking. Perhaps, when we do that, we're trying to write our way into the present moment, to be contemporaneous with our own thoughts." That's part of the logic that underwrites swerving in syntax. (It is also what I am trying to do here.) Hank Lazer, discussing Armantrout's "swerving," the sudden turns and redirections of sentence and thought in her poetry, quotes Lyn Hejinian on metonymy: "Metonymic thinking moves more rapidly and less predictably than metaphors permit—but the metonym is not metaphor's opposite. Metonymy moves restlessly, through an associative network in which the associations are compressed rather than elaborated." But probably metonymy plays no greater role in Armantrout's poetry than analogy does; her "thinking of thinking" has less to do with the nominalist ethos that underlies metonymic practice (as in the poetry of William Carlos Williams) than it has to do with her suspicion of available logics. Armantrout's work is not especially rich in particulars, after all, less rich than Raworth's, for instance. It is closer to Marjorie Welish's work, with its interest in the limits of logical systems. The first poem in *Next Life* ends as follows:

> To quick-step up the street
> in a knit red cap
> one time only
>
> ★
>
> Red cap is to
> one time only
> as

It might help to think about the first stanza by imagining it prefaced by "How great or special it would be," in order to make a complete sentence. That sentence would express the desire for singular experience. The next stanza is "about" how that detail of the red cap relates to "one time only," preparing an analogy that the poem refuses to complete. We are left to imagine how the sentence *could* be completed: "Red cap" is to "one time only" as a sharp detail in a poem is to the poem's singularity. Of course by completing that sentence we contain the meaning of the poem in a proposition and make it less interesting. Elsewhere in *Next Life* we have poems that are "about" the word "as": "*As* keeps it coming, / keeps us company. . . ." If that's not fast enough or too pedestrian in its quasi-personification of the word "as" inside this metaphor, try this, the opening couplet of "Promise": "Canary yellow of the school bus; / school bus yellow of the SUV." What for many other poets would be simple description becomes for Armantrout investigation of the way we describe.

Driving back to the hotel in Louisville after dinner with Diane at Lily's on Bardstown Road, I hear on the local classical music station an old interview with Sir Thomas Beecham, talking about his friend Sibelius: it's the 50th anniversary of the composer's death. Beecham has a bunch of anecdotes about Sibelius to share. Sibelius liked cigars, he says, and smoked cigars bigger than the ones Winston Churchill smoked. It was not so long ago that few critics thought of the great Finn's music as interesting, but I don't care about that and promise myself I'll buy a Sibelius CD at earX-tacy on our way out of town. I do a little reading online and find a reference to one biography and see that it has an anecdote about the composer's death that Beecham hasn't relayed. Sibelius was a bird-watcher, a lover of the outdoors. At the age of 91, he was walking one day when, as the biographer reports, he saw a flock of cranes flying above: "Here they come," Sibelius told his wife, "the birds of my youth." Then one crane pulled out of formation and circled above him, before returning to the flock. Two days later Sibelius died of a brain hemorrhage.

The Irish poet Maurice Scully inserts an anecdote about Sibelius in his book *Over & Through*, included in his collection *livelihood*. The anecdote's author is the composer's wife. Scully lineates the anecdote as a poem, inserting it after his poem "Sound":

A Personal Note

Music irritated my husband more than
anything else. Forced to hear a stray
tune, a fragment of song, or someone
whistling, he would throw his work
overboard and wreck the inspiration.
Afterwards he must begin again from the
beginning. That is why at home one never
heard music. No one ever sang. No one
whistled. That is, unless my husband
chose otherwise.

It hardly matters what kind of asshole Sibelius might
have been, or how conservative his music is. One
can certainly understand the *need* for a classical composer whose music is accessible, at least as accessible as
good food, not that good food is that easy to find. It's
why we're in Louisville, in fact. Meals are prepared
at Lily's with attention to detail, but without pretension. That makes it one of Diane's favorite restaurants;
cooking is her art form. The wait staff doesn't bat an
eye when the couple at the table beside us, spotting
Diane's digital camera, offers to take our photograph.
Not a word about how invasive this is, no effort to
control the environment. If Sibelius was a control
freak, as Scully's poem shows us, he took a beating for
decades at the hands of culture snobs like Adorno—
there's no controlling that. In more recent years his
music has come back into style, finding critics who
think of him much as Stravinsky did at the end, which
is to say respectfully. No controlling that either. But
it's pleasant to encounter a level of competence and
care for one's craft without an accompanying pretension. We'd been remarking all day on the friendliness

of Louisville as a community, where even the homeless wish you "good morning," as if compelled by etiquette unknown just two hours north and east in Cincinnati.

Two million plastic bottles are used in the US every five minutes. 130 million cellphones a year are discarded. A collection of anecdotes might seem a small thing.

Ahmadinejad lectures at Columbia; Cubs up three and a half with a week to go. Some days there is no keeping up, only the sense of something one can't name creeping forward, as if futility shared a root with future. Today I want the proverbial hut, the place away from places hut, the get the fuck away from me hut, the let me off this couldn't be slower as a rickshaw hut, the beach party hut with tedious music like the music on Steve Earle's latest CD, the really far-away hut, the tropical breeze no matter how seedy the surroundings and impoverished hut, the seeds already irradiated I'm eating the vegetables anyway hut, Martin Heidegger's hut, the missiles tipped with tactical nuclear warheads missing somewhere in the skies over Florida hut, the hope to hope hut, the hut after the latest holocaust of consumerism third world blotto with a roof, with a good space heater. I don't want to move to New York like Steve Earle, get fatter, release a CD with new songs that sound like the good old songs without their energy. I don't want to do it again. I don't want to sit around and wait to think of something, thinking of nothing is a good thing, better memories of nothing much, turn it down it's like a bloody ukulele, a role on an HBO series? It doesn't matter. God bless you Steve stop by the hut any time I'll put on Jimmy Buffett, one of his execrably familiar tunes. I don't want to be an immigrant in my hut, the hut must be a permanent home. I don't want to move to Philadelphia where the mob runs the trash racket and the Russians run the mob and they say Americans have no culture and no history. I'll make a hut of twigs and dollars, remaindered copies of William Butler Yeats. I won't be walled in here in the home of the grave, this damp sewer of a world and outer space wasted by celestial trash. Put my hut on nowhere island open to wind and error. Put it where it really blows.

Callers

I thought I knew about goldfish memory. Or I believed what I'd heard about their three-second memory, until I read about the latest research on goldfish. Then I wanted to know if I could still tell the joke about the goldfish dropped in the ten-gallon tank. You know the one. The goldfish is introduced to its new tank. It looks around and thinks, in the way that a goldfish thinks, "Nice tank." Three seconds later, it thinks again: "Nice tank." This goes on: "Nice tank. Nice tank. Nice tank." That's a joke better told than written down. But the truth is no joke: goldfish have a memory span of up to three months, and fish have other signs of intelligence too. They can feel pain, or that's the theory, which, now that I read about it, reminds me of Frank Bidart's translation of Catullus's "Odi et amo," which inserts a phrase about the fish who wants the fly even while dangling from the hook.

Cubs drop three in a row to Marlins but ride into the playoffs with a win over the Reds. At Great America Ballpark, the stands are full of blue, Cubs blue. A man stands up two rows in front of us (my students Rachel Smith and Ben Kuebrick are to my right) and says "Boo Cubbies, boo Cubbies." Soriano leads off with a homer and later guns down a runner trying to score from second base on a single. Back in Oxford, Bill Howe drops a vinegar bottle on his foot and reacts to the tetanus shot; my colleague

Cathy Wagner comes down with flu on the eve of her guest Rae Armantrout's arrival on campus. The next day Diane and I catch another game and later watch customers remove their shoes at the Korean restaurant in Covington. It's the day after the Cubs clinch, the day before Diane's birthday. I have two beers in the Deadwood saloon next door to the restaurant, sawdust on its floor, the bar decorated with huge posters from the greatest television show ever made. How I miss that sepia epic! The dead are fed to pigs owned by the Chinese boss. He likes the English word "cocksuckers," which is counterpoint to the pseudo-Shakespearean eloquence of the show's white protagonists in their monologues.

I had been thinking of titles for imaginary poetry books: *Fall and All* might be appropriate for the century *after* the American century. And also of the titles of real books: *Caller*, the title of Tom Raworth's latest, means what? Is it "caller" as in "gentleman caller," and without the modifier more ominous? I decide for the moment that the title refers to the "caller" that is death. I don't know if it's true, as Freud says somewhere, that we are incapable of imagining our own death, but it seems true that some people have, or come to develop, a sense of their own mortality more powerful than what others develop. Everybody knows that older people, with more experience of death, have a different posture toward mortality, a sense of human finitude that shapes their everyday life in subtle and not so subtle ways. It might be that I have not met anyone with a stronger sense of mortality than Tom Raworth, the Raworth I met when he was not yet sixty as much as the Raworth of today, at seventy. This could be seen beside his hedonism and the speed and intensity that accompany pretty much everything he does, from reading his poems to eating his meals. There is, in his person as also his poems, an impish wit accompanied by skepticism about knowledge claims. In his work, where precision is *of the moment*, he can be joyful even—he is surely funny—about the way time erodes knowledge. From one point of view that is our best hope, it seems to me—discovering that what we know is not enough, not even close. No doubt there are any number of biographical facts one might point to by way of explaining some of this about Raworth—his growing up during the Blitz after being born with a hole in his heart, the early death of his beloved daughter Lisa, endless medical trauma, and so on. But I am not interested in explanations, only anecdotes. I was sitting next to Raworth at Trevor Joyce's house at the SoundEye poetry festival in Cork one year when, Joyce having put on music by a blind Delta blues player, Raworth leaned over and said, "I don't mind dying." Was he citing the blues? Another time, after he read in Oxford, I drove him to the airport for his flight out west. We were making small talk about Carolyn Forché—I'd just been to DC and seen her at an event at Bridge Street Books—when Raworth said "This could be the last time" and flipped the little book he'd just signed into the back seat. Any number of moments like this might explain why I am tempted to read the title of *Caller* the way I do. But the last time I saw Raworth, he told me, as if to defeat my assumptions again, as he has so often before, "There will always be another time." So much for anecdotes; they escape their frames. *Caller*'s juxtaposition of word and phrase, its word and phrase collocations,

won't allow its reader a place to stop until—well,
until one stops:

> there's only one of you
> mere sight of kind nomadic
>
> cue there goes god
> set them shone
> meaning few in their suites
>
> fire of thought
> why work for afraid
> rather than angry
>
> human decoration
> resisted in every way
>
> not the general good
> round deaths up or down
> to tidy
>
> the best for each other
> next year in jerusalem
>
> don't mind us
> go on with your war
> we're for lost city

All of Raworth's poetry is obsessed with time.
"Caller" might be the poem *most* obsessed with *mortality*. But that's only a distinction forced up by this
writing, and even as I write the sentence I am aware
that "caller" could refer to a person on the phone—
remembering Raworth's job many years ago as a
transatlantic telephone operator, where he would

overhear and assist "callers" in several languages. The ability to plug in and overhear fragments of many conversations, to remember and mimic idioms from many discourses, has always been important to his poetry.

If a book of anecdotes is something like Pound's rag-bag—one can toss anything in—it's time I put in this bag its oldest seed, those few anecdotes I published a few years ago in *Jacket* concerning Raworth:

'till mute attention / Struck my listning Ear'

Memory of standing in line at G & W Carryout in Oxford, Ohio: Tom needs razors. Then to the post-office to express mail Peter Green's new translation of Apollonius's *The Argonautika* to Ed Dorn, who had just given it to Tom in Denver: Ed, pushing against his illness, needs it back to move ahead with work. Here at the house asked by Diane if any of the knick-knacks caught his eye: the two glass bottles, he says, simple reds and greens, late winter sun on them, a buck each at Odd Lots. The lamp with five globes curving close to the ceiling: 'I've always found it difficult to get enough reading light overhead.' A carved street rat from Bali, its defiant and comic pose. Later, listening to a CD of poetry and music: 'The music wins every time.' No need much for words, whistling maybe, or whistling along, a smile of recognition is four or five volumes. Posture as given in the first poem of *Tottering State*: 'Waiting.' In Cambridge a plate of cold cuts, olives, cheese, Val animated, skewering the pretensions of many. Generosity to youth in too many locations to detail, cigarettes under New Hampshire greenery staving off overkill readings at Assembling Alternatives. Uncomfortable, shy to be asked to explain collages at a party in Chicago: Tom turns to a few of us listening and says 'John Cage lives!' Navigating complex turns to Bill Fuller's house in Winnetka after drinks on the north side that same night: just as soon as I'm sure this can't be right we're there. A glass of water after reading through *Writing* at the University of Chicago, back for another twenty-five minutes from *Meadow*. More formal get-up on Tom new to me: makes me feel better about having spent two hours talking about his work to Bob von Hallberg's seminar, saying things like 'If this were another century Tom would be our finest epigrammatist and miniaturist. But since it's after that time the work is necessarily more oblique, spun in deft turning, that kind of observation, detail, and comment every bit as cut and cutting but in pieces and rearranged.' I left out the wonder of and in it, the anger too. What's ever said about the poetry that's up to the poetry if the poetry is up to anything at all? We must try. Another moment in Cambridge: 'Nobody ever notices my *rhyming*.'

Time's almost up: scratch again. What to offer Tom Raworth to match the surprise of his poems? What to do to thank him for community delicately threaded by his necessary — fated more than fêted — travels? Time to fetch the Apollonius book from the library maybe. No way Tom got past Book I on the jet. A few lines from Book III then: 'Medeia could not remove her thoughts to other matters / whatever games she might play: not a one that she embarked on / caught her attention for long. She quickly found them boring, / kept helplessly chopping and changing…' I don't know anything about Medeia's story, haven't read the book. That's what caught my eye flipping through. It occurs to me that Tom might have a few lessons for Medeia in the possibilities of boredom and distraction as modes of attention. Or maybe not. Argonaut and Argot-naught both.

I should have said humming rather than whistling—it's more typical of him. But much of this still seems right. Many times I have heard Raworth dodge questions about his method of composition, but when he does say something about it, cutting is usually what he talks about—how he cuts until he can cut no more, this happening in his head rather than after the fact of the writing.

"Not every poet wants to be a philosopher king," I say to Rae Armantrout in the car on our way to Cincinnati, kidding her about how the poems in her book *Next Life* are impossibly intellectual and self-reflexive, every word a pressure cooker. We're on our way down to Cincinnati for lunch at the Korean restaurant and to see the city, Aaren Yandrich joining us. I haven't been yet so decide to check out the Freedom Center on the river beside the stadiums. It's a new museum about the history of the Underground Railroad. Like the Museum of Science and Industry in Chicago, it turns out to be a museum for people who don't want to read much, housing a few artifacts of the period but featuring lots of videos and interactive exhibits and video games. What decisions would *you* make as an escaped slave? Would you try to escape in winter, fall, or summer? Stick to the rivers or keep along the back roads? Would you trust that candle you see in the window? No matter— you're right in every case and never caught by the dogs. A video narrated by Oprah Winfrey introduces a surround sound movie in a theater made up like a riverside forest. On the way back I ask Armantrout about *The Grand Piano*, the multi-volume collective autobiography by and about some of the language poets in their early years. She says, "I'm running out of memories of the seventies."

The night after Armantrout's reading, my sister Karen calls to tell me my mother has been taken by EMS to the hospital. She'd been at Karen's house and talking as she talks of late, the threads of her conversation fraying. When dinner was over, it was obvious that she was not able to walk, Karen says, as if she'd had a small stroke, her head in an unusual position, pushed down at an angle against her shoulder like the late pope's in the last days of his Parkinson's disease. Karen is convinced that she has Parkinson's. This has been missed for months, she says, the doctor having diagnosed her with a mild form of dementia. In the hospital, a team of doctors recommends Trazodone (sleeping pills) and Lorazepam (an anti-psychotic). My mother spends the evening raving at my father and sisters and everybody else in the room, hallucinating, making as if she were writing on a chalkboard—she had been an elementary school teacher. It is disturbing to hear about this, to say the least, as my mother is a woman who never has a bad word for anyone, a quiet woman of Scots-Irish-Puritan-Midwestern-Lutheran-Methodist farmer stock, a touch of iron in her as in the well water on her family farm. "I like people," she said to me when I saw her on my way back from Buffalo.

By the time I get to the hospital the following morning after the five-hour drive north, my mother is a little better, and she improves throughout the day. My father uses the occasion of my hanging around in the hospital lounge to reminisce, and he tells me how my mother has been doing in the weeks since I last saw her. Her loss of appetite has increased—she's lost fifty pounds over the course of six months. Meanwhile he is remembering his own mother's biological father, divorced by his grandmother at an early age. I ask him what this Mr. Schott did for a living. "He was a wastrel," my father says, using a word I've never used. He describes his step-grandfather, Mr. Langham, a gentle man who took him fishing and cared for him after the wastrel was mostly out of the picture, and while his paternal grandfather, Mr. Tuma, and his own father were busy drinking with the Irish in Cleveland. He tells me about episodes from his youth I've heard about before—the time he worked in Cleveland's Harvard Club, notorious as a mob hangout, machine-guns stashed behind the paintings above the bar. He tells me about his father, Stanley, who was born outside in the snow one Christmas Day in Cleveland and pronounced dead, who waited to correct the official record until he was ready to marry, having confessed to his bride-to-be Helen that his real name was Stanley Tuma and not, as she thought, Martin Gallagher—close family always called him Marty. Some of this is new to me, some not. He tells me what the fortuneteller said at the department store in downtown Akron when he went with a friend from work to have his fortune told and the fortuneteller told my fortune too. He tells me he has been "pure as the driven snow" for almost fifty years of marriage, after the loss of his virginity in Havana during World War II, which he also tells me about—about two older soldiers who told him not to come back to the barracks until he got laid, after finding him a French-Cuban whore. He is telling me all this, I think, in order to keep from having to talk with me about his fears for my mother, fears he knows I share. He is telling me this to try to be a good father, which I already know he is. He is telling me this as his way of showing me that he's loved my mother but also that he will be okay if my mother has to spend time in a nursing home. He is making up stories about how he will go on if he has to go on without her. His father Marty, he reminds me, visited whores at the track after my grandmother died, taking a cab after his cataracts prevented him from driving. "He needed a woman," my father says. He is tired, I think. So am I.

As the day goes by my mother improves a little: her thrashing, her picking at gown and blanket slows. I talk to one doctor who seems to have no clue about what is going on; he is the psychologist. I tell him that I want my mother taken off the heavier sedatives and anti-psychotic medicine. He agrees to see to this, and I believe that he will. Two days later, I am home in Oxford and hear from my sisters that my mother is doped up and completely non-responsive, in a delirium that might be drug-induced, nobody knows.

The night before I leave Akron I sit in my parents'

kitchen and watch the Cubs lose their third in a row to the Diamondbacks, Ramirez going hitless for the series. For breakfast in the morning, my father thinks we should try Bob Evans, but there is a wait, and we stand in the parking lot until he decides that we should go across the street to the Subway in the Wal-Mart—he and mom eat there often, he says. "Those are fall clouds," he says, as we get in our cars. Then to the hospital, where we make small talk with my mother for a few hours since she is more alert and responsive, if sometimes confused. Mostly she just listens. To have something to talk about while we sit with her, I try to tell my father a little about my book of anecdotes, and my mother chimes in with—we stop conversation for her every remark— "Keep writing." After two hours, I give her a kiss, tell her I love her, and make her promise me she'll eat something. Then it's the five-hour drive home. I pull into town at 6:30 with the sun in my eyes, the warmest October on record, evening coming in over the wheat and cornfields off 732. Three or four farmers are harvesting their crops, one of them kicking up a lot of dust, another coming at me on the road in his giant combine. I pull over to let him pass.

These are my mother's drugs: Haldol, Trazodone, Inderal, aspirin, Aricept, Namenda, Lopressor, Tapazole, and Seraquel. My sisters email me the list and convince the doctors, as I thought I had already convinced them, to take my mother off sedatives and anti-psychotics. Later we learn that she has been on 5 mg of Haldol when the recommended dose (the drug is not often recommended for the elderly) is .5 mg.

Back in Akron at the hospital, sitting in my mother's room, I read Nate Dorward on Trevor Joyce's *Syzygy* ahead of Joyce's visit to Oxford. It is day four of my mother's delirium: she's semi-conscious, unresponsive, apart from the occasional one-word answer and her moaning. She's pulling off her hospital gown, her legs churning as if to paddle one of the little boats Diane and I used to watch on the Lincoln Park lagoon. "*Syzygy* has an idiosyncratic bipartite structure" and owes something to Guillaume de Machaut's setting of the text "Ma fin est dans ma commencement" ("My end is in my beginning") in a crab canon. The crab canon is a composition in which "one or more parts proceed normally, while the imitating voice or voices give out the melody backwards." There is nothing I can do for my mother. I take a break from Dorward's essay and head out for coffee in the lounge. A tall black man in a hospital gown peeks out the door of the next room to see who's in the lounge and speaks to a white woman who is telling somebody on a cellphone that "the cancer in the spine has spread." The woman is not listening, so he turns to talk with me. He has had two brain surgeries for cancer, and a third because "Somebody thought I had money and bashed my head." He is smiling. "God must have a purpose for me," he says. "Count your blessings, young man," he says.

Deciding to return to Oxford, leaving my mother in the hospital with the plan for her care still uncertain, I hope for the best-case scenario, her release to a nursing home or rehab center. Diane and I have tickets for Elvis Costello and Bob Dylan on Tuesday, and the night after that Trevor Joyce is coming to town for four days. I've been reading Mark Slobin's remarks about what he calls the "superculture" in *Subcultural Sounds: Micromusics of the West*, a book I've been meaning to read for years and finally have pulled off the shelf. Slobin wrestles with his skepticism about various terminologies and his own provisional category "superculture," which he defines as "an overarching, dominating—if not domineering—mainstream [culture] that is *internalized* in the consciousness of governments, industry, subcultures, and individuals as ideology." Slobin is uneasy with the word "hegemony"—"how do you know hegemony when you see it?" He explains his preference for the "truly nebulous term" *superculture*: "It implies an umbrellalike, overarching structure that could be present anywhere in the system—ideology or practice, concept or performance. The usual, the accepted, the statistically lopsided, the commercially successful, the statutory, the regulated, the most visible: these all belong to the superculture." The components of a superculture in music include an "industry" and its alliances with media and technology. Its hegemony, Slobin writes, is "neither monolithic nor uniform" but allows for "alternative and oppositional voices." The state has a role in shaping the superculture, as for instance by designating the boyhood home of Lawrence Welk a museum. As I read this, I remember that the Lawrence Welk show was what my family watched in the evenings at my maternal grandparents' house after we played softball with our cousins and had our meal, my mother's father sitting in his rocking chair beside the radiator talking with the adults, the rest of us up close to the screen, not particularly interested. Bob Dylan is a part of the superculture too, I think, a much bigger monument than Lawrence Welk. Does this mean that I have been had? That I am now a part of the machine, co-opted, to use the word my Marxist friends used to use? Has Bob Dylan done this to me and to others, or have we done this to Bob Dylan? I remember the presidential award presented him by Bill Clinton, the singing of "Blowin' in the Wind" as a kind of kumbaya in elementary schools, even in my day. But I also remember that it was listening to records like *Highway 61 Revisited* and *Blonde on Blonde* on Jeff Norris's porch when I was 15 that first gave me the idea that I wanted to read and write poetry, or maybe it was Dylan and Jeff and his Dostoevsky and Nietzsche and Pynchon and Ginsberg and Blake, excerpts from each scrawled on the wall of his room at the top of his parents' house. I am remembering how most of what I got into in those days, especially the dope, disappointed my mother. And I am remembering a few moments of low comedy years later with Dylan still around as a soundtrack to my life—cracking up while having sex and hearing the phrase "It's a hard" repeating in the chorus of "A Hard Rain's A-Gonna Fall." Now Dylan's playing with Elvis Costello at the Nutter Center at Wright State University in Dayton, and Diane and I are there and not at the hospital. It's great to see Elvis for the first time and Dylan for—what—the tenth? We're in the seventh row, close enough to see their eyes. The tickets have set me back 300 bucks and I am only partly into the scene, less so when I see several older colleagues from the university sitting a few rows in front of us. I suppose they offer me an uncomfortable reflection. I listen as Elvis asks the crowd to help him as he sings (shouts) "Wake up," meaning that we should be paying attention to what President Bush is doing to the country. The crowd is happy to oblige, though slow on the uptake. Elvis tells the crowd that he must be doing all right to be playing shows after all these years—and with Bob Dylan tonight. Then it's Dylan himself in a broad-brimmed hat and black suit. He plays "Rainy Day Women #12 & 35" and, fourteen songs later, ends his set with "Masters of War." The arrangement is heavy with drums, almost Celtic. He plays the guitar because his keyboard has stopped working during the previous song, to be replaced later for two predictable encores. I am happy the keyboard is broken. For a minute, watching him make it up on the guitar, it is possible to lose myself enough to believe in the music.

The last time Trevor Joyce came to town, he read with the English poet John Wilkinson. There was one day when I left them to wander the trails in the woods behind the art museum while I took care of business in the chair's office. Trevor, John, and also Chris Hamilton-Emery, an English poet and publisher who was in town for something else, managed to get lost—the trails are a little confusing, though marked with signs. The three of them eventually made their way to a clearing and saw the art museum ahead, where I had promised to retrieve them. At this point, Wilkinson said to the others, "There it is. Let's walk up and rest on the sward and wait for Keith."

When I heard about Wilkinson's remark, I thought that it might have been the first time the word "sward" had been used outside of a poem in Oxford, Ohio since the university was founded in 1809. In America, the word belongs exclusively to *poetry*, an antiquated poetry at that, and Wilkinson's use of the word speaks volumes about his Englishness, as also about a studied eloquence that his poetry often challenges, even as it can't help but be eloquent. I can't remember if he read this poem from *Contrivances*, a poem about lyric, but it will serve for an example:

The Line of Reinforcement

Catch it again pluck, sounded flat.
The skeining soon repairs
melodically strewing rosy parts
uncaught, uneventfully.
Central demands stay viable but
neatly disposed of.
O falter, o buy a fatter duvet
not to put too fine a catch.

Apple-bobbing I kept my head.
Riding the king's
highway came no cropper, relay
yards of silk, calmly.
So wherefore the hair in the tooth
flexes the tongue or
dull down waves of sun-spasm
vary the all-in-all?

That's the catch catches nothing
remotely. Cries may sound
dissociated, thick pond
grant no wish, then in a flash
a crowd forms for a fire-eater,
& over stainless surfaces
accompanied song skids
straight to the heart's clutches.

Does it make sense to read this as a poem about musicality, about control and abandon? If so, Shakespearean eloquence and "faltering" are both allowed by this verse even as it hardly falters. The poem seems to admit the possibility that something in or about a poem that the poet does not altogether control—though the poet might shape the poem perfectly—will "skid" and collide with a reader. The poet's job, however, is to perfect the poem rather than to worry about that, about the reader or listener. "Catch it again pluck" (is that Shakespeare?) might be paraphrased as "Get the tune right." The poem cuts and turns quickly, but it has room for a "wherefore" as also for the variation on "came a cropper."

While he was in town Wilkinson talked about the difference between his work and the work of the language poets. "Their work has no inside," he said as we walked around the corner by Buffalo Wild Wings, "and mine has no outside." I think he might have meant that the work of the language poets has, in theory, rejected the models of literary subjectivity that operate in mainstream poetry, models of the self and its representation or expression in poetry. As for what it means to "have no outside" to a poem, that's much harder to say, but, since Wilkinson is unwilling to include the reader in his idea of the poem, as a lot of language poetry tries to do, maybe it's that. In an essay, he writes that "the poem can achieve completion without circulation or publication, a phenomenon sharply indicative of the disjunction of the aesthetic domain from ordinary human commerce." In another essay, he writes that he wants to "make a cursive and ahistorical claim for the unconscious drives." Put these propositions together and one arguably has—sometimes has—a hermetic poetry in which subjectivity is not flattened in public discourse but is instead a black hole where embodied mind grapples with what is beyond its understanding. In "The Line of Reinforcement," the body is a site of dissonance and imperfection, of the stutter that makes for song, "the hair in the tooth." The line is difficult to paraphrase, complex: "That's the catch catches nothing / remotely." There is the sound-play of "catch" and "catches," but is it that no thing—nothing—is caught, or rather that nothing is caught except at a distance (remotely), as in a tune heard across the distance of years? There's that eloquence again, the sound of *tradition*: the posture of this verse will appear Olympian beside the pratfalls of most varieties of a more *distributed* language poetry.

"He thinks I'm gloomy," Trevor Joyce tells Cathy Wagner as we drive over to the bar after the reading, referring to my introduction. I was speaking about the poems, not the person, but Joyce does have his moods. I first saw him flat on his back in the hotel room where he was rooming with cris cheek and Allen Fisher at Romana Huk's Assembling Alternatives Conference in New Hampshire, an Irish poet I'd barely heard of put in with two English poets I had come along with my old friend Alan Golding to meet at this most important of conferences. He had his sleep mask on, wiped out, resting after a series of all-nighters trouble-shooting for Apple Computer. But he was soon up and ready to talk and ready to re-enter the poetry world with his first book in many years and a couple of bottles of whisky on the table at the end of his bed. Jump ahead eight years, and there's this same Joyce, who by this point has published *with the first dream of fire they hunt the cold*, one of the most impressive volumes of collected poems to appear in recent years, running down the stairs of his house in Cork at 2 a.m. It's after a night of partying at his house following a day of the SoundEye festival, the festival he's kept alive for years to sustain the spirit of transatlantic and international exchange begun at Assembling Alternatives. Trevor's house is really the center of the festival. He's out in the street in a flash. Before the rest of us know it, he has a drunk and obnoxious poetry critic in a headlock, said critic having made an asshole out of himself by shattering a plate glass window because he was angry at having been booted from the party for forcing his girlfriend to sing one too many Irish songs for a group of us. (When the glass shards crashed into the living room, narrowly missing a few of us sitting at a table, Tom Raworth was the first to spring to his feet to follow Joyce out the door: "Now we're going to have to *kill* him.") Or there's the memory of Trevor striding ahead of the crowd up and down the hills of Cork—this could be any year— leading people to the various reading venues of his festival, thin as a rail, manic, his comebacks in conversation fast as a train. His poems are archetypal, their speakers impersonal, as Fanny Howe notes, and they are Irish in one sense that the other, more famous Joyce's work is Irish, which is to say learned, without being cowed by knowledge. There's "The Turlough" too and respect for the Irish landscape, its idiosyncrasies and history, respect for Irish life and tradition, but one is as likely to be in the neighborhood of Genghis Khan or the Chinese poet Ruan Ji in reading a Joyce poem or translation. It's all part of the mix he works with.

In the last decade Joyce's poems have gathered and churned texts most of us have never heard of, arranging them in stark collages, or running them through neo–oulipian procedures. It could be a poem by an early T'ang poet, a Finno–Ugric folk song, or one of his own 36-word lyrics: Joyce has the whole conference of birds in his head, and the lyric impulse first and foremost:

    Like last year's
    winter wheat my hair
    scarcely sprouted
    and was shorn.

    Like green timber
    my soft bones
    scarcely sprouted
    and were shorn.

Bones are a favorite image—"the red noise of bones" is a phrase in his poem *Syzygy* and the title of his CD. Life is brief and hard in these poems, known by all to be so—that could be the Famine as it lingers. It is also the wisdom of folk songs from many lands, many languages, where song and music are likened to the rattling of bones and instruments are fashioned out of the hair of drowned maidens fished out of rivers. The simple parallelisms and turns of a folk song like the one above are there in "Kindling" too, a poem altogether Joyce's own but which already sounds centuries old, such is its resonance:

    i put wood in the fire
    when no one was about

now there's fire in the wood
and i can't put it out

And the idiom of this short poem is the same idiom used in many of the 36-word poems of *What's in Store*:

the marvellous
bird
won't sing
on every
branch

i don't
always have
a quilted
bed

pity me
wait for me
turn to me
kiss me
pity me

red apple
eating
straw bale
sleeping

turn to me

This one reminds me a little of Ode 28 from Basil Bunting's *First Book of Odes*, a "working" of a poem by the Persian poet Hafez as a blues tune. Like that poem, Joyce's begins by establishing a pattern via repeating syntactic structures, the first and second stanzas parallel. It syncopates that beat with something like a bridge—and then we're on to a new pattern.

Not all of these intellectually fast 36-word poems by Joyce use a similarly archetypal, bones and wood and apples diction. There's this one, for instance, which begins with a familiar metaphor but soon eschews image for statement. It is almost a handbook about the use of the stanza to push a poem forward, the turns between the first and the second stanzas and between the penultimate and last as tight as any in the history of poetry:

storm
across
the mind
dismays
this one

thought is
precipitate
is always
incompleted

fragments
disperse quite
unavailable
to memory

yet it must
somehow pull
itself together

name
birth
address
reasons
forms are
to be
filled out

If the idea of thought fragmenting and fraying is depressing enough, as also the tedium of bureaucratic forms filled out, this depression isn't unique to Ireland. But *Buile Suibhne* is, and it might be the ur-source of the aforementioned "gloom." It was translated by Joyce as *The Poems of Sweeny, Peregrine*:

I am miserable
Sweeny,
bone and blood
are dead;
sleepless;
storm-sound
is the only music.

Cathy Wagner says something like, "Well, the poems *are* pretty gloomy," and I ask Joyce about this translation and the status of the "storm-sound" in Irish poetry, about whether or not some of his tropes and tones might be traced back to this medieval text, and about whether or not these can still be used in a contemporary poem. "You can use them now all right, because Flann O'Brien has already taken the piss out of them."

Three hawks make a figure 8 above a shorn field off to the left as I drive out to the park to walk

Milo. Powerful birds, no wind against them. At the park, I count 19 black vultures in a tree by the pet beach. Odd to think of vultures in a flock, if that's the right word, to think of them as social like that. They prefer one tree by the edge of the lake. I have seen them here before, the tree leafless now ahead of the others around it. That and the fact that the vultures are brown allow them to pass for hawks, I suppose, but they are too big to be hawks. One sits atop the beach house, two on the sign that reads "Public Beach Unguarded." I'm thinking of nothing at all. The pet beach is beside the public beach, with its patch of sand, on a jetty with a duck blind that's made up a little tiki. Milo and I walk out to it, and I sit on a picnic table as he wades into the ripples of shore water. Not far off an old woman with bright hair walks her dog; she'll wave later as she drives off, happy that someone else has found this place to walk a dog on a fall afternoon, before the rain blows in. The vultures are so many and large, too large for these branches, and noisy flapping between branches. There was something in my mother's voice yesterday, something soft—weaker, but for the first time in weeks lucid— the voice of someone who has been very ill and come back changed, on the mend. "I've been better," she says when I ask her how she is. My sisters tell me she doesn't remember my presence at her bedside in the hospital. She's calling from my sister's house; she's out on a day pass from the rehab facility, or they call it that. For others it is a nursing home. One sister tells me about the place, and that my mother spoke to one of the older women zonked out in the lobby. "This old lady was holding a plastic doll like it was her own child," Kathy tells me. "Mom says, 'What's your baby's name?' to her.

She says 'Baby.'" "Parents please watch your children," the sign says at the beach. A man in his early 30s, with a ponytail and yellow shirt, jogs by. Milo roots around in the brush under the tree holding the vultures. It's the day after the Indians lose to the Red Sox, which must be good news for the networks. There's noise from a single-engine airplane above, and a singer on the radio singing the old chestnut "I hear you knocking but you can't come in. Go back where you been."

Then the news on the telephone: my mother is dead, having choked to death on her breakfast at the nursing home, the rehabilitation center. My sisters and father will make the funeral arrangements and call me back. Outside the window of my study the brightest tree in the backyard has dumped about one third of its orange leaves—every other tree is intact and green. It happens this time every year. I wonder how long my mother had to suffer, alone in her room, searching for air. I try not to think about it.

Then I wonder how many doctors I can choke with my own hands. Haldol is to be used with great care in the elderly, the online medical journal recommends. After they are persuaded to take my mother off the antipsychotics, it's four days to cycle them out of her system. Then she is free of them but agitated again, more restless than ever. "What should I do, Kathy?" she keeps asking, trying to get up. She can't get up, though; she's too feeble to walk. "Pray for me, Kathy." So they keep her attached to alarms out at the nurses' desk. Then there's word that she's been misdiagnosed with a hypothyroid problem; her problem is the opposite, hyperthyroidism: she's been cranked in the wrong direction. Kathy and Karen are frosted, to use an expression invented around the year they were born. But then it's over, I think. She's on the mend.

"Dead is dead," Tom Raworth wrote me once, after the loss of one of his many writer friends. It wasn't Ed Dorn—someone else. I'm not sure what he meant. Perhaps it was that, with a loved one's death, and with the possibility of real conversation with that person gone, the books—as it were—are closed. You can write in the book, you continue to write in the book, but it's not the same. At the same time there is no closure, no end really. Already the tenses blur. What does it matter what I told my mother, since I won't be able to tell it to her again?

Late in the day, happier news: my mother did not choke to death. The preliminary results of the autopsy are in. Her death was painless and instantaneous—the cause a dissected aorta. It's not enough, but it's something.

We don't understand the king, the Brits say, meaning King Abdullah of Saudi Arabia, as the Queen and high government officials wine and dine him at the palace. He says the British don't do enough about terrorism, meaning King Abdullah's enemies, and that the British ignored his government's warnings before July 2005. We don't know what he's talking about, say the British, and how dare he say that. But we'll talk to him. There's the money and the trade and the oil and the power—you've got to belly up at the bar with somebody. I think of the prose text at the bottom of one section of Dorn's "Languedoc Variorum" where Dorn says that they're all in it together, the really big money people, regardless of creed, color, or nationality. There was the 40 billion pound arms deal the Office of Serious Fraud was investigating until that was called off in the name of the national interest. That's another nation, not my own. After the King leaves London, he will stop in Germany, Italy, and Turkey.

In her coffin, my mother is pinked up, rosy. She was paler in life, slow to anger and slow to joy, steady in her love and in her fellowship. Now she is rubbery to the touch, though I might be the only person during calling hours who touches her corpse. 250 callers. My sisters and my father greet them all, and I do too, standing at the end of the line. I'm happy to be at the end of the line to have to say the least. There's my mom's friend from down the block, whose son was a better gymnast—our picture in our stretch pants was in a local paper when we were in elementary school. Years later he shot himself in her basement. My mother was the friend of most of these people— my first grade teacher, looking exactly the same forty years on, the woman from two doors down whose tomboy daughter several of my young companions had crushes on. Then there are the church people. One of them tells me that he lost his parents decades ago and it still seems like yesterday. At the service the next day, the woman minister quotes the Bible about wearing the apron of humility, which seems right for my mother. I learn a few things about her at the service and from her friends. Then it's back on the road—Allison has classes the next day and we must get home. Near the exit at Eaton on I-70, I pull up behind a black hearse somebody has made his own, spending the extra dosh for plates that read DEADSLD. I imagine ramming him, and then remember it is two days before Halloween. My mother would pass out candy to the neighborhood kids, smiling. I see her rolling her eyes in mock disdain.

You think you're over it and then you're not, like they say. The wind goeth toward the south, and turneth about toward the north: it whirleth about continually: and the wind returneth again according to his circuits. Another warm day in this long fall, and I am out at the lake again, walking to treat my sore back and think. Three or four boats are still docked; one boat is out on the lake. I sit on a bench and watch three gulls, then four and five and six and more, twenty yards out over the water, diving for food. Diving isn't the right word for what they're doing, however. They stop and hover above the water for a second, a letter C with wings, then back up into the wind before plunging into the lake. They aren't heavy or strong enough to dive deep, and though I sit and watch them for half an hour until the wake from the boat chases them down the shore, I don't see one of them with a fish in its beak. I won't make a metaphor of this.

John Cage is one of the great anecdotalists in American literature. His interest in the anecdote is shared by many other writers and artists who, like Cage himself, belong to the avant-garde, from Apollinaire (*Les Anecdotiques*) to Daniel Spoerri (*An Anecdoted Topography of Chance*) to fiction writers such as Lydia Davis, whose title story in *Samuel Johnson Is Indignant* might be a joke about anecdotes. But whereas Spoerri and his collaborators describe 80 objects lying on a table on October 17, 1961 at exactly 3:47 p.m. and the stories or memories these objects suggest, building those memories via collaboration, most of Cage's anecdotes are not the product of experimental method or process but instead conventional auto-biographical stories, including stories about Cage's career as composer and aesthetician. Cage inserts the anecdotes between chapters of his book of essays, *Silence* (1961), and does much the same in its sequel, *A Year from Monday* (1969), printing the anecdotes in a small font. The anecdotes are a thread binding the book's other contents, situating the work in a life, a life made small beside the work or essays about the work. The content of the anecdotes can be as ordinary as this description of family life:

> I was arguing with Mother. I turned to Dad. He spoke. "Son John, your mother is always right, even when she's wrong."

That's funny as the kind of thing one can imagine being said by nearly any father in nearly any family. Other anecdotes, as for example an anecdote about Cage's success as a teenage radio host, and several about his mother and father, memorialize the idiosyncrasies of the artist and his family. There are anecdotes about his life as an amateur mycologist, detailing his passion for hunting, studying, discussing, and eating mushrooms. These range from statements of "interesting" facts he has discovered about the use of mushrooms—"On Yap Island phosphorescent fungi are used as hair ornaments for moonlight dances"—to more elaborate accounts of his experience with and conversations about mushrooms, including an anecdote about Ohio mushrooms and

Yellow Springs, Ohio, home of Antioch College, an hour northeast of Oxford. It is easy to see how anecdotes are *like* mushrooms; the best of them pop up at the bottom of more imposing structures beginning to rot. Still other anecdotes describe incidents in Cage's working life as a musician and performer, or the conversations that accompanied that life. Friends and colleagues such as David Tudor and Merce Cunningham often appear. Cage likes the artist anecdote for its ability to demystify the artist. He includes one anecdote about Franz Kline's mother showing up at the opening to an exhibition of his black and white paintings and saying to her son, "Franz, I might have known you'd find the easy way." This is parallel to another about Cage's mother in which she tells him that she's "not fussy about music" and then that "You're not fussy about music either." A few of the anecdotes sketch Cage's aesthetic views and his practice as an artist, reporting something that someone like Mies van der Rohe once said and Cage's opinion about the statement, or discussing a performance such as *Music Walk* vis-à-vis "indeterminacy." There are a few anecdotes about historical figures such as Meister Eckhardt. This combining of the personal and the philosophical and the historical perhaps deserves the name "American," but there are anecdotes that aren't American in the least. There is one borrowed from, or re-telling, an Irish myth. There are numerous anecdotes that concern Cage's study of Zen Buddhism, including the following:

> Another monk was walking along when he came to a lady who was sitting by the path weeping. "What's the matter?" he said. She said, sobbing, "I have lost my only child." He hit her

over the head and said, "There, that'll give you something to cry about."

Okay, then: one thing after another. Let's get on with it.

Of God, Man, and Animals

Musharraf declares martial law, shuts off the phone lines and television. The Bulls, listless, drop their first two games. It's how to do it again that I can't figure. The little things I can manage—get up and walk the dog, etc. Being on leave allows me time to grieve, time most who grieve can't afford. On the radio coming back from the park there's a story about a man who worked on the HBO show *The Sopranos*. His mother was brutally murdered 30 years ago, raped and murdered, and he's obsessed about it since. He keeps weapons throughout his house, a sword here, a baseball bat with a nail there; he's done it since he was a kid. Once he wanted to breed rats to turn them loose on intruders, but his father nixed that idea. He was in therapy for years, he says, but he doesn't talk about it. The crime was solved long ago. He wants to solve it again for himself, trying to prove his improbable theory that the murder was not random, despite evidence long in hand. His apartment in NYC has three deadbolt locks and a chain. For *The Sopranos* he worked scouting locations for murder scenes. The interview ends by noting that, for now, he's given up on making a documentary about his mother's murder and plans to open a restaurant in the city.

In news from the world of science, the UK government rethinks its laws about human hybrid experiments, or so I read. If they're approved, new regulations will allow for human–animal hybrids, including "cytoplasmic" embryos, which are 99.9% human, and "true hybrids" carrying both human and animal genes. "Chimeras" made of a mosaic-like mix of cells from different species, and "human transgenic embryos"—human embryos modified with animal DNA — will also be allowed. I wonder if this is good news for baboon society, which is matrilineal, with eight or nine matrilines in each troop, each with a rank order. The hierarchy can remain stable for generations. By contrast, the male hierarchy, which consists largely of baboons born in other troops, is always changing. Males fight amongst themselves and with new arrivals. Rank among female baboons is hereditary, with a daughter assuming her mother's rank. This provides great satisfaction to a member of the British royal family. She tells researchers in Botswana, "I always knew that when people who aren't like us claim that hereditary rank is not part of human nature, they must be wrong. Now you've given me evolutionary proof!" (http://www.nytimes. com/2007/10/09/science/09babo.html)

I think it's about time to get back to reading and so head over to King Library to get a book I've been wanting to read for a year or so, Giorgio Agamben's *The Open: Man and Animal*, which is about the production of ideas of the human as that has involved ideas of the animal: "The anthropological machine of humanism is an ironic apparatus that verifies the absence of a nature proper to *Homo*, holding him suspended between a celestial and a terrestrial nature, between animal and human—and, thus, his being always less and more than himself." The book begins with Agamben considering several drawings of human figures with animal heads, as found in a thirteenth-century Hebrew Bible in the Ambrosian Library in Milan, and then moves into discussion of Hegel's end of history as interpreted by Kojève and Bataille. He takes up the work of Linnaeus, the zoologist Jakob von Uexküll, Heidegger, Benjamin and others. I am hoping that he will tell me something I don't know or haven't read about in the work of Erica Fudge and others about the relationship of man and animal, but for the most part he doesn't. He closes with a reading of a Gnostic text by Basilides that proposes an "idea of this natural life that is unsavable and that has been completely abandoned by every spiritual element—and yet, because of the 'great ignorance,' is nonetheless perfectly blessed." The pataphysician Alfred Jarry is name-checked as Agamben writes that "It is not easy to think this figure—whether new or very ancient—of the life that shines in the 'saved night' of nature's (and, in particular, human nature's) eternal, unsavable survival after it has definitively bid farewell to the *logos* and to its own history. It is no longer human, because it has perfectly forgotten every rational element, every project for mastering its animal life; but if animality had been defined precisely by its poverty in world [the usage is Heidegger's] and by its obscure expectation of a revelation and a salvation, then this life cannot be called animal either." Agamben's is a messianic materialism wherein both animal and human are "outside of being." Somehow, it's not enough, not for me, it's too depressing and too familiar. I had expected something more than another articulation of the so-called post-human, more than a discourse apparently convinced that we are or should be through with "the word," with *logos*. I guess I'd expected something with—how to put it—a little less certainty about its own propositions, especially those that involve not-knowing! And the book is positively a hymn to not-knowing: "The righteous with animal heads in the Ambrosian [Library] do not represent a new declension of the man-animal relation so much as a figure of the 'great ignorance' which lets both of them be outside of being, saved precisely in their being unsavable. Perhaps there is still a way in which living beings can sit at the messianic banquet of the righteous without taking on a historical task and without setting the anthropological machine into action."

Reading Agamben's book, I think of Clayton Eshleman, who has been preoccupied with similar questions for many years. His work is informed by many of the same sources—Bataille for instance—though also by James Hillman and others who have written about animals and dreams. Eshleman's emphasis is often on the Upper Paleolithic as a moment of crisis, a definitive (though he agrees with Agamben that it is not the final) separating out of "man" from an animal nature, a moment that for him is also the beginning of image making. I hope that I am doing the claims he makes in books like *Juniper Fuse* justice. Eshleman finds in the cave paintings at Lascaux evidence of "the astonishing ancientness of the human creative impulse" and hopes that these paintings as "discovered in this most inhuman century" might "somehow offset total despair." There is obviously a personal dimension to this for Eshleman, as one can see in his speculation (based on Barbara Macleod's testimony relating her quasi-mystical experience in a cave) about the possibility of connecting with the energy of the cave: "It is as if the soul of an all-devouring monster earth could be contacted in cavern dark as a living and fathomless reservoir of psychic force."

It's been years now, but I used to see Eshleman now and again. Somewhere I have a photograph of Clayton and his wife Caryl sitting on our couch, covered with the stuffed animals a tiny Allison had brought out of her room for them to see: Big Bird, Cookie Monster, others without copyrighted names. And one year he served me a dinner of rabbit in saffron at his house in Ypsilanti. In her book *Animal*, where Fudge discusses anthropocentrism and the animal as pet as opposed to the animal as source of food and clothing, there is a passage where she talks about her difficulty, as a child, eating the rabbit pie her mother served (while calling it "chicken pie"): "For me, the rabbit was an animal to be petted, not potted." The rabbit in saffron Eshleman served me was my first (and last) rabbit, and, while I was not a child, I remember the same difficulty. For me Eshleman has always been someone who has forced confrontations with uncomfortable realities like this. There is no denying his energy, the massive *work* he's done, in and for poetry, as a translator, as the editor of two of the most important poetry magazines of the later twentieth century, *Caterpillar* and *Sulfur*. But there are many challenges in dealing with his intensity: he can be brutally honest. To his credit, this same honesty is visited upon his own life and history in his poems.

Reading Norman Malcolm's book *Wittgenstein: A Religious Point of View*, I am struck by a conversation Malcolm reports between the philosopher and his friend Maurice Drury. Wittgenstein tells Drury,

"It is my belief that only if you try to be helpful to other people will you in the end find your way to God." I believe in being helpful, in that much at least. And I also find myself imagining that I know what Wittgenstein is talking about in his "Lecture on Ethics" when he speaks of a moment in Vienna when he suddenly felt "*absolutely* safe" and experienced the "state of mind in which one is inclined to say 'I am safe, nothing can injure me.'" In suggesting that there are ways that Wittgenstein's philosophy is analogous to religious thinking, Malcolm links this feeling, and Wittgenstein's statement about it, with Psalm 23: "Yea, though I walk through the valley of the shadow of death, I will fear no evil: for thou art with me." Once or twice I have thought I might know a little about this feeling. I suppose part of that is an anecdote my parents used to tell me—I have no memory of the event myself, apart from their story—about something that happened to me as a young boy on my Grandfather Elder's farm. My grandfather had taken me to see a cow with her new calf. When the door to the barn was opened for me to see the calf, the cow freaked out, probably at the sight of the toy gun I was carrying. It charged and knocked me down, then did a crazy cow dance around my head, without harming me, except for a small cut above one eye. There is a Faulkner story that describes much the same kind of thing, though it is a raging horse the small boy in the Faulkner story blissfully ignores. Then, too, there is the anecdote about Alexander Pope and the cow. I might have been dead then and there but somehow made it through. I can name other close calls, as everyone can, events that I remember, in cars for instance, where I was lucky or somehow blessed not to have it end right there, and I can remember friends and family talking about similar events. In World War II, working as a radio operator in planes patrolling the Panama Canal, my father once had to prepare to parachute into the ocean as the engines in his plane threatened to quit—the pilot managed to limp back to base with one engine. You're always lucky, until you're not, and then you're not around to talk about it, so maybe you're always lucky. Or some are. The harder task is to understand those who feel themselves to be perpetually unsafe.

Now it's the memory of Lorenzo Thomas at the Diversity in African American Poetry Conference in Oxford in 2003. He has survived lung cancer, but emphysema is killing him, which he must know at some level but doesn't mention to me. Instead we talk about LBJ's old friend Frank Oltorf, whose name comes up because I have given him a copy of a book about Tom Raworth's poetry that Nate Dorward has recently published and which includes Raworth's "Sic Him Oltorf!" Thomas and Raworth knew each other in Texas, and Thomas tells me stories about those days. It is not anything about the stories that I remember but rather his happiness, the sense of a man at peace with the world, happy to be there sitting in the sun outside the conference center. A year later I am finishing the editing of *Rainbow Darkness*, an anthology containing poems and essays by the people who took part in the conference, so I write Thomas to have him sign off on page proofs for his poems. He does that, and he doesn't bother to mention that he's in hospice care. He's dead two days later.

Downtown Boom

There are no gospel singers
Anymore

On the corners
They held down for Jesus
Valets park cars
At restaurants for fancy people
On expense accts or dates

So many times
People come up to me
And say, Billy
Hey wait a minute
You not Billy!

You can see the new ballpark
Just past the Courthouse

But which way is redemption?

The contrast of ballpark and courthouse, street preachers and rich people in Houston—it's just perfect. We think we see somebody we know—"Billy." We don't.

Bulls lose five out of their first six, lose to Toronto by nearly 40 points. Musharraf quotes Abraham Lincoln; lawyers are jailed; Bhutto is under house arrest. Markets as stable as my stomach after too much chipotle. I'm out to the lake again as the November light warms the air, imitating late September, a third of the leaves red and orange, enough to paint the shore. On the road coming in the other direction I see an eccentric bicycle, its rider helmeted and sitting low and reclining to pedal, reminding me of an old man in Indianapolis Diane and I saw last year atop one of those funky bicycles you see in museums, a penny-farthing from the early twentieth century, with a huge front wheel and a tiny rear wheel, the rider sitting five feet in the air so that you are left to wonder how he got up there in the first place, and what happens if he topples over.

Out of Line

I have been reading *New York Times* columnist Frank Rich on "The Coup at Home," an op-ed about how the freedoms Americans once enjoyed have been taken away in the last seven years, possibly never to be restored, and remembering a reading Tom Raworth gave at the university in the weeks following the election of George W. Bush to his first term. Hanging chads were still an issue, the election itself. At the end of his reading, Raworth pulled out his Parisian music box, which he used in those days to conclude readings. He'd punch holes in a card strip to spell out a word, sometimes several words, and run this card through his music box to play a tune, his slow turning of the crank producing music that contrasted with his high-speed, non-stop reading. I can't remember the word that was cut into the card for this reading—"performance" perhaps, as Raworth was reading after cris cheek—but I remember that he had the left-over confetti in an envelope, which he then produced from the pocket of his jacket. "This is for the coup you all have just experienced," he said, dumping the chads on the floor.

As we stand in line waiting to see the Mountain Goats at the Mad Hatter in Covington, it's obvious to Diane and me that we're old enough to be the parents of most of the kids attending the show. Our daughter Allison is older than some of the kids. In front of us are three girls with their faces inked heavily and haircuts from 1968, boys with soft sideburns—middle-class kids, most of them from over the river in Ohio. It doesn't worry me that I am an old fart at the concert. This crowd, maybe 150 people, is a sign that the Mountain Goats aren't going anywhere, though their music is better than ever with a drummer added to the mix and the bass of Peter Hughes pushing the guitar and vocals of John Darnielle. The band has found its niche in small clubs and university towns; Covington isn't typical in this regard. The music is maybe a little too tweedy, the nerd edge of post-folk, of so-called "weird America," but I like it. Diane asks me if this is the kind of bar where kids come to hook up. I doubt it, though I find out later that it once was a strip club, which explains the black carpet and pink lights. Darnielle, his voice pitched near boy soprano, wears a sport coat for the show. The show is short and terrific, concluding with a song I don't know that I think might be called "House Guest," the lyrics of which are typical of Darnielle's songs in refusing rock and folk music's more predictable tropes. "It's not dark yet," Bob Dylan writes. "I'll be a good house guest," Darnielle replies. The lack of pretension is refreshing. It's true that many of the songs sound the same, their lyrics interchangeable. I think it was 1996 when my student Rich Housh put me on to a couple of cassettes by the Goats, including *Zopilote Machine* (1994), where Darnielle's undergraduate training in classics at Duke University shows up in songs like "Young Caesar 2000," a persona poem in the voice of a petulant boy emperor. So it turns out that they've been around since some of the kids at this show in Covington were just out of diapers. Part of the attraction of their music then was its DIY production values; the first recordings sounded like they were made in a living room with a cheap micro-phone and cassette recorder. Lo-fi they called it. But some of the songs were (and are) remarkable. There's "Going to Scotland," one of many "going to" songs about places I suspect Darnielle hadn't been to when he wrote them. There's "Waving at You." There's "Wild Sage" and "Woke Up New" on *Get Lonely* (2006), which leaves lo-fi behind for the studio. These are all pop songs in a line that includes singer-song-writers like Mayo Thompson and Jonathan Richman and Tamas Wells, among others. It's a line as familiar as the lines on my hands.

In the dream I'm back at my elementary school for the day, doing what I'm not sure, though at one point I am observing, or preparing to observe, two small boys in white t-shirts and shorts about to play a game of one-on-one basketball. The backboards and baskets are antique, far more antique than the baskets at my elementary school, hung too low, and yet somehow it is my elementary school. The gym, which does not resemble the gym of the school I attended, has sloped floors, like the floors in one corner of the top floor of the new Cincinnati Museum of Contemporary Art. One basket dips almost out of sight at the gym's far end. There is a table, as if meant for taking tickets, and although I don't see anybody sitting at it I know its chair is meant for a woman. Earlier, or possibly later in the dream, I am jogging by this same elemen-tary school noticing that there is a priest in its front window, or a minister. I see his collar, and somehow I learn that he is at the school to talk about its dress code. In the middle of this dream I am hearing a fierce screed by the young English poet Jow Lindsay concerning events in a tiny, mostly invisible part of the poetry world in the UK. Lindsay is describing poetry readings and related events, and what I have to do with what he is discussing is unclear. By the time I am ready to wake from the dream, the gym is empty, the two boys gone off somewhere, and I decide to pick up a basketball to heave it at the far basket. As it hits the backboard the ball explodes in a thousand pieces of paper. This part of the dream, I determine later, owes something to a commercial I have viewed many times while watching NBA games. The paper floats to the ground like the trash of a roman candle. I get up and open the blinds in my study. There's a dusting of snow, the first snow of the year, on the ground. I am 50. On the *Drudge Report* it says that the Pope contemplates banning modern music; Gregorian chant is once again popular. It says that the Chinese have told hotel managers in Beijing to make sure they stock condoms in every room for the Olympics. There are many other stories, Drudge punching his euros into the hydrogen jukebox of American fantasy.

Diane and I go down to the Esquire Theater in Cincinnati to see Todd Haynes' "biopic"—odd coinage, too close to biopsy—about Bob Dylan, *I'm Not There*. Cate Blanchett is brilliant in it, having learned the nuances of Dylan's gestures, posture, and speech, and the movie is striking visually, as for instance in its only sex scene, and in the opening, where the camera pans along what might be a Manhattan street examining face after face, all of them fit for a freak show. And maybe the freak show is where Haynes wants to locate Dylan. The movie assumes its viewer has extensive knowledge of Dylan's career and the legends that have circulated about it, and thus it's no surprise that it was much discussed in the press before its release—those stories had to be reprised for the benefit of those who had forgotten them. Newspaper reporters and bloggers did the movie that favor. Some film clips of Dylan that are part of the archive are visually cited in the film, images from *Don't Look Back* and from Dylan's performance in Manchester, others that Martin Scorsese used in his PBS Dylan documentary. There is a homemade surrealism about several sequences in the movie, especially the sequence about Dylan at the Newport Folk Festival, where the effect of Dylan's going electric is imagined as the band turning machine guns on the audience while the festival curator tries to hack off power to the stage, cutting the cable with an axe. Or maybe it's unfair to surrealism to call those sequences surrealist. Of all the phases or periods in Dylan's career, Haynes is least convincing trying to represent the melancholy that has characterized Dylan's music in recent years, the period Richard Gere's character represents in the movie. Better-known earlier Dylan personas offer Blanchett and the young black actor-singer Marcus Carl Franklin an advantage over Gere. The Gere character also seems to fold in the Rolling Thunder Revue in one scene that takes place on the edges of a country circus, with animals wandering across the set and a painted barker and a patriarch with a pistol. It's an odd scene, as if out of *The Confidence Man*, and visually indebted to *Renaldo and Clara* and other footage of the Rolling Thunder Revue, as well as the cover image from *The Basement Tapes*. Despite the supposed fluidity of Dylan's identity, which the film wants to insist upon, it seems that Haynes has a pretty good idea of the Dylan that matters most to him, a cross between Arthur Rimbaud and P. T. Barnum. The movie concludes with an image of Dylan playing

the harmonica, which might be the only real footage
of Dylan used in the movie. Dylan is playing his circus
organ licks on "Mr. Tambourine Man," I think it is,
blowing up and down and up and down the keys,
circling the chord.

Now I am listening to Luc Ferrari's *Les Anecdotiques*
while writing down a few memories of our trip to
Chicago to see the Bulls play the Atlanta Hawks.
Ferrari's liner notes state that he subtitled his classic
musique concrète work *Hétérozygote* "anecdotal music"
with "an intentional touch of derision." He writes
of "three planes" in his musical composition. The
first is everyday sounds recorded in a particular place:
"the project was to seize the opportunity offered me
by a number of travels. . . . I recorded what I found
interesting." These ambient sounds are mixed with a
"second plane," electronic sounds he found unused
in his archives, and a "third plane" of "spontaneous
and intimate" words, conversations with women he
recorded long ago. I have the CD courtesy of the Jazz
Record Mart on N. Wabash, a fantastic jazz music store
in Chicago. We'd stopped to shop the day after the
game, and I bought CDs by David Grubbs, Andrew
Bird, Albert Ayler, Steve Lacy, the Art Ensemble of
Chicago, Peter Brötzmann, the Sun Ra Arkestra, and
Ayuo, among others. Earlier we'd wandered our old
neighborhoods, Lakeview and Lincoln Park, noticing how many of the shops along Broadway north
of Diversey had changed in the twenty years since
we'd walked along that street. The Dominic's grocery
store is a concrete slab waiting for something to be
built atop it. The sex shop called The Pleasure Chest
is gone, as is the family-run gyros and moussaka joint
across the street from our old apartment. Stella's Diner

is pretty much all that remains, the little boutique on Briar Place called The Purple Cow is gone, the small drugstore on the corner of Briar and Broadway is now a Japanese restaurant. Lots of Middle Eastern restaurants, a mediocre new used bookstore where I buy Henry Green's memoir *Pack My Bag*. South of Diversey, we walk past an old woman begging on the street: I give her some change. As I do so a man in a trench coat and winter gear—it's cold enough that we don't want to walk too far—says to us, "She'll spend it on a ticket," meaning a lottery ticket, speaking with an air of certainty that suggests he knows her well. We walk along the street with him for fifty yards and discover that he does know her, has known her for twenty years he says, and knows that she is "obsessed" with one particular numbers game. He speaks as if the woman is an old lover, in tones of exasperation and resignation. Diane comments that this is what living in this neighborhood must mean, knowing people; he's been here twenty years, which is to say since we left. We wonder what he thinks of the Turkish restaurant called Cousins. For the game we take a cab through the yellow underworld of Lower Wacker Drive to the United Center, where two jazz bands, one playing music dating from the '40s and the other a small post-bop ensemble, entertain fans in the mezzanine. They make for a happy mix of nostalgia and anticipation as we move through the crowd. We find our seats in the sixth row behind one backboard and succumb to the bright strips of video screen surrounding the court, the surround sound, the JumboTron hanging above the court where we can watch what we can't see with the backboard obscuring our view. We are close enough to hear Luol Deng say "C'mon" to his teammates. Next to us is a young man in a

Dennis Rodman jersey with a wig version of Ben Wallace's afro, hollering loudly enough to attract the attention of the players on the bench. He wants the Bulls to stop shooting jumpers, to take the ball to the basket; he wants the two rookies put in the game. The video screens with their messages periodically whip up the crowd. Diane snaps a few photos of the young man, asking his permission to do so. "Sure," he says, "if you'll email them to me." He gives us his card; he's a real estate salesman, a little older than Allison. It's a bad market, but he's come to this game. At halftime we wander around a little, and I stop in the john to discover that there's a poster advertising something above each urinal—each urinal a billboard. The game over, we see the clean-up crew ready to work, five or six Mexican kids with brooms and mops passing us as we leave the court and head out into the street. The cab driver who dropped us off at the United Center had said there would be cabs lined up after the game, but we don't see a single cab. We wait a half hour before we manage to grab a private car, with the help of the same guy we saw on our way in. He had asked us if we would help an unemployed vet. We'd crossed the street to ignore him. Now he flags an unmarked cab he knows about, and we give him a dollar.

I am beginning to feel like John Wieners in his *A Book of Prophecies*, listing "Poets I Have Met." I won't list or discuss them all, I hope. There's Andrew Duncan, sitting among a group of British poets around the huge oak table in the Senate House on Malet Street in London. I'm there to talk about Eric Mottram, and Duncan is hunched over the table taking notes in tiny handwriting in his tiny notebook. He comes up to me after the talk and says he has no idea why I think that anything important is ever going to happen at Dartington College of the Arts, where a new performance writing program has recently been established. There's Ed Dorn at Alan Golding's place telling me that Ted Hughes is a more interesting poet than Thom Gunn, or, years later, across the table in a restaurant out on the water in Bar Harbor, talking about yuppies walking their cougars on the devil strips of Boulder. I tell him I am writing about English poetry; he says it's all English poetry as far as he's concerned. Now it's Richard Howard's visits to Oxford—or the first of several visits, when he came up from the University of Cincinnati to lecture about something or other, about translating Proust maybe, and gave the lecture in pink slippers. On another occasion I am introducing Frank Bidart, who is to read his brand-new long poem "The First Hour of the Night," and I see Howard sitting in the front row. Bidart reads the poem and heads directly over to Howard to ask him what he thought of it, as if Howard's is the only opinion in the room that matters, as well it might have been, since Howard had chosen Bidart's first book, *Golden State,* for publication in an important series. Howard doesn't seem altogether convinced by the poem, and later back at the inn I find myself pointing Bidart to the phonebank so he can call Howard in Cincinnati for more details concerning his reaction. Now it's Robert Pinsky drinking tea at the house, signing a book to Allison "from your father's friend." We'd met in Chicago and exchanged a note or two in my days at the *Chicago Review*, probably concerning Jim Powell, whose first book I gave to Alan Shapiro and Bob von Hallberg, who published it at the University of Chicago Press. I haven't spoken with Powell in more than twenty years, but three days before I write this we are visiting a bookstore in Hyde Park and I think I see someone who looks like him together with someone who looks like his friend, the distinguished Latinist W.R. Johnson. It's curious what I can connect with what—too little, really. Now it's John Ashbery in Rod Mengham's study at Jesus College, Cambridge, after Ashbery read there with James Tate. Some of us are talking on the other side of the room, ignoring him, when suddenly Ashbery announces that he is leaving and says, "Please don't talk about me when I've gone."

Harryette Mullen has been to Oxford to read twice, most recently for the African American poetry festival that featured Lorenzo Thomas and many others. A gentler soul has never lived, a kinder smile. I remember telling her that Allison, not yet a teenager when I met Mullen on an earlier visit, protested every time I threatened to shave my head, this being an obvious solution to the fact that most of my hair has fallen out. "Your head is shaped like an egg," Allison would say, "It will look terrible." I told this to Harryette, and she said, "You have a beautiful skull," which is just about the nicest thing anyone has ever said to me. But it crossed my mind later that, as a scholar of nineteenth-century American literature, she might well have been thinking about the brutal uses to which phrenology was put in the racist pseudo-science of that period. The legacies of racism are right there in the most ordinary places:

Kills bugs dead. Redundancy is syntactical overkill. A pinprick of peace at the end of the tunnel of a nightmare night in a roach motel.

Their noise infects the dream. In black kitchens
they foul the food, walk on bodies as we sleep
over oceans of pirate flags. Skull and crossbones,
they crunch like candy. When we die they will
eat us, unless we kill them first. Invest in better
mousetraps. Take no prisoners on board ship, to
rock the boat, to violate our beds with pesti-
lence. We dream the dream of extirpation. Wipe
out a species, with God on our side. Annihilate
the insects. Sterilize the filthy vermin.

That's a poem from her book *S*PeRM**K*T*. It
begins with the famous advertising tag line for the bug
spray Raid. (Ron Silliman likes to say that this slogan
was authored by the poet Lew Welch.) The other
bug spray in the poem is Black Flag, which for a long
time had a flag with a pirate's skull and crossbones as
part of its label. Surely no funnier poem about the
Middle Passage has ever been written, which doesn't
make the poem any less serious. Reference to suburban racist clichés concerning cockroach-infested
African American kitchens and to racist discourses
about sterilization and sending African Americans
back to Africa—it's not so far from the nineteenth
century to the present.

Another of Mullen's poem from *S*PeRM**K*T*
begins "Off the pig, ya dig?" That line in turn always
reminds me—no doubt my readers will soon tire of
these memories—of something Amiri Baraka said
when he was in Oxford to read. This was soon after
Miles Davis died, so Baraka read his elegy for Miles—
in a chemistry lecture hall with giant posters of the
periodic table hanging behind him. Baraka pounded
the podium and hummed a few bars of "So What"

and went off into the poem—a powerful reading, 300 students spellbound. He'd come to life faster than Frosty the Snowman for this performance, after sleeping most of the afternoon at the university guest-house, since his morning flight to Oxford had followed an early morning in New York. He'd been up at 2 a.m. to drive from Newark into the city for an interview with Australian television about Spike Lee's film *Malcolm X*, which he didn't care for. He was nodding off now and again during our conversation on the long drive from the Cincinnati airport in Kentucky up Route 27 to Oxford. I had the local college radio station on low, and he came out of a nap to say, "What *is* this? Geriatric jazz?" That was perfect, as I'd always thought that the station's jazz deejay, Mama Jazz, greatly esteemed by locals for her knowledge of jazz history and for the gravel in her voice, ought to be made to play something recorded after 1945. Before the reading we went to dinner, where as part of a conversation I mostly forget I was talking about how I'd met Muhammad Ali at a conference about Ali's life and career held at the university earlier that year and hosted by my friend, the sports historian Elliott Gorn. I added that I thought I'd once seen Ali when we were living in Hyde Park, Chicago. I was walking along 53rd Street; he was in a limo picking up food at Ribs & Bibs, at 53rd and Dorchester. This led Baraka to a story about his own favorite ribs joint in Newark. There are often very long lines, he said, and he'd often contemplated yelling "All right, all you Muslims, out of line!"

Now it's Tony Lopez, at breakfast, like the rest of us a little ruffled after a late-night party, handing me his new book of poems—this was Dorf Tirol and my first

Pound conference. He wants to know if I will review it. Sure, I say, and tuck the book in my bag. It's Lee Ann Brown and Kristin Prevallet singing a duet in the wee hours of the morning at a conference in Orono, prompting Alan Golding to sing in a big voice I can barely believe is his an English drinking song, with David Bromige and Stephen Cope and Tom Orange around the table, Sylvester Pollet and George Bowering too. It's Leslie Scalapino after I ask her about a cushion she is carrying around at Assembling Alternatives—I am thinking the cushion might assist her meditation, knowing of her interest in Buddhism: "It's for my back. It's killing me." It's Jimmy Santiago Baca telling students at the university about his friendship with Denver Broncos quarterback John Elway, and then asking them about the difference between film (he'd written a script) and literature. "Celluloid," a smart-ass on the faculty answers. It's Turner Cassity, Donald Davie, and John Hollander lined up against a wall at Bob von Hallberg's apartment in Chicago, and as I try to enter the conversation Hollander says to Davie it's time to go—but Davie stays to chat with me a few minutes, even though I have nothing to say that's likely to interest him. Or it's years later at an MLA where I'm on an upper floor of a hotel when the elevator opens and there's Hollander again, alone, riding down. I decide I'll make a pain in the ass out of myself and pretend we're old friends, though I know he doesn't know me. "John!" I say. He's uncomfortable, grunts hello, asks me what I'm working on. I list a bunch of poets I think he doesn't greatly respect—Basil Bunting, Hugh MacDiarmid, George Oppen, others—and talk about my work as if I know he will be fascinated by it for the full minute and a half of a slow ride down, many stops, to the ground floor.

He meets a friend at the bottom and I watch them turning around to glance back at me as they walk off ahead.

Dead cat's bounce in stock market, sucker's rally: now it's not whether there will be a recession but whether it will be a soft or hard landing and how long it will continue. God is only 6,000 years old, Régis Debray says: "For he was not always there, above our heads or in our hearts. There was a time, a very long time, during which He was nowhere to be seen; and another, quite recent, in which that void was duly registered or alleged." If I type Gog instead, this book gets shorter. "Someone who will die for you and more. It ain't me, babe," the voice on the iPod says. Oprah on the road for Obama; Chavez in red shirt at rally. Evel Knievel dies, of diabetes and pulmonary thrombosis. Israel forces the withdrawal of an American-authored U.N. draft resolution after an Annapolis sit-down. U.S. Military Sealift Command tenders extra tankers to move jet fuel from Diego Garcia to the Gulf. Russia prepares to vote, all eyes on Putin. First cold snap of December. My father puts up his Christmas tree.

Of the Avant-Garde and Its Others

It is not only the avant-garde poets of Britain that I have met. The late Michael Donaghy, whose contributions to poetry are remembered in a lecture established by organizers of a conference sympathetic to what Michael's friend Don Paterson calls "mainstream" poetry, was my friend in Chicago, before he moved to the UK. He had dropped out of the master's program at the university before I arrived in town. I met him at a meeting of the *Chicago Review* editorial board, on which we both served for a time. Michael reacted badly to official coursework at the university and also picked up a serious dislike for the poetry of Charles Olson. To the end of his life, he was given to dropping gratuitous remarks about how Olson was a fool and academics bad for poetry. In those days Michael wasn't always sure about what to do with his life, or so it seemed, though one thing that pleased him was playing traditional Irish music with his friends, including a very good fiddler who came down from Milwaukee now and again. It's piano that I have sometimes tried to play, but one night I sat in on bongos at the house on Blackstone Avenue where Michael had a basement apartment. That was the instrument available—Michael played tin whistle and bodhran. It was the big party for Michael's leave-taking. He had decided to give up on Chicago and follow his girlfriend, Maddy Paxman, to London. For several years leading up to that night, we had discussed poetry, particularly British and Irish poetry. Michael especially knew about Irish poetry. Thanks to University of Chicago professor Frank Kinnahan, we both met a few Irish poets as they came to town. We met Paul Muldoon at a party, and Michael Longley and Seamus Heaney read at the university. Longley and Heaney I remember as pleasant company; Muldoon I chatted with only briefly. I went with Tom Bonnell to fetch Heaney at O'Hare, where we managed to forget where we'd parked our car and wandered the parking deck for half an hour looking for it: Heaney was gracious about it. We took him to the Berghoff in the Loop for lunch. He didn't want to talk about poetry. He bought Dunhill cigarettes at the airport from a young woman who asked him about his accent. Later he read to one of the biggest crowds I have ever seen at a poetry reading, with locals, Irish-Americans maybe, lined up for a hundred yards outside the doors of Swift Hall waiting to get in. Michael was studying the work of these poets, and we were talking about them and about other poets such as Basil Bunting whose work interested me more. At the *Chicago Review* we were all a little tired of the limp free verse of American poetry and looking for alternatives. Michael was interested in the work of James Merrill and Richard Wilbur and the possibilities of so-called traditional form.

Michael was said to have a heart problem and had already lost one or possibly both of his Irish-American parents. His early poems were not so far from what later became known as New Formalist poetry. They were "wiry" little poems, as Donald Davie wrote in a blurb for *Slivers* (1985), a book published in Chicago shortly before Michael left the country, small poems emphasizing intellectual wit and working a central trope in the manner that some used to call "metaphysical." I remember that "Machines" was one of them. It's a poem he's still remembered for in anthologies. In a balanced and slightly ceremonial syntax, the poem proposes a similarity between Purcell's harpsichord music and a racer's twelve-speed bike in order to define the operations of grace—poise—for an absent lover who is also, of course, the reader. The poem is ultimately concerned with grace as a property of poetry itself.

When Michael moved to the UK, he became friends with Don Paterson and Sean O'Brien and others who already were or were soon to be plugged into the poetry establishment in control of *Poetry Review* and other mainstream publications. Soon he was an Oxford poet and publishing articles lambasting American poets for their ignorance of meter. He was made part of the promotional hoopla that gave England its "New Generation" poets. Poets were dressed in black clothes for photo shoots; they were to be the new rock n' roll. These poets, Michael included, pooh-poohed this as nonsense, but publication and careers were on the line. The promotion set the poets up to be skewered by the avant-garde and anybody who was paying attention, but it worked to establish them at the center of British poetry culture. Having achieved this level of recognition, which meant awards like the Forward Prize, which comes with a fair chunk of change, Michael and his friends hoped their work would be of interest to academic critics, though Michael knew that, in the United States, academics were writing about language poetry. So

I wasn't surprised when nearly the first thing that he said to me when I saw him for the first time in ten years was, "What is it going to take to get a little academic attention for this poetry?" I was in London for an academic poetry conference. Michael had graciously invited me to a reading and party at a place called The Pirate Castle in Camden Town. I arrived too late for the reading, but Michael introduced me to some of the people at the party as the dancing was starting. I felt immediately that this was not my crowd but did my best with a little schmoozing. Some of them had been told I was editing a poetry anthology for Oxford University Press—they would not have known that this was to be published out of the New York office. I noticed that nobody I spoke with had heard of the British poets who interested me the most. I remember mentioning Raworth, Prynne, Maggie O'Sullivan, Allen Fisher, Denise Riley, Tom Leonard, and various others to a few people as we were smoking on the roof. One older woman, a kind Anglo-Cuban poet named Jane Duran, had heard of Raworth and said that she ought to stop in to see what he was up to in Cambridge these days. Somebody else said, "That's Ken Smith's crowd." Downstairs I saw somebody who looked like Don Paterson skulking around the edges of a few conversations. Michael still had the broad boyish grin I remembered. He introduced me to a young Anglo-Iranian poet who was thrilled that her first published poem was to appear in a London newspaper the following morning. Would I come with the group to a club later? No, I wouldn't, I had things to do tomorrow, shopping for a Beanie Baby Allison wanted. But I did dance with Michael. We paired off like a couple of ridiculous gunfighters, and the small group around us seemed to like that.

Soon the crowd was thinning out and, at midnight, a little man came around and turned off the lights. I heard from Michael several times afterwards as I was working on the anthology. He sent me a book on prosody he wrote with a grant he had from the lottery money the English were passing out in those days to put poets in law firms and zoos. I didn't know what to say about such a manifesto. A few years later, there was news of his death, at fifty, and now there is the sense of a friendship lost to stupid poetry politics.

An email from Tom Raworth comes in telling of his Christmas visit with J. H. Prynne and daughter, the exchange of gifts, "port and pudding for biscuits." "Not a word about poetry nor literature was uttered. But we had a laugh." Prynne's gift was "the last summer apple (D'Arcy Spice)" from his garden. I ask Raworth if he *really* wants to eat that apple, and get a few more details: "It's a late cropper, can be picked in November and stores until April . . . the original <?> tree was found in the grounds of Tolleshunt D'Arcy House, in Essex, in 1880." The story reminds me of another I heard from him about plucking a rose from Pound's gravesite on San Michele in Venice to send via express mail to the dying Ed Dorn. Shown the rose, Dorn tried to eat it. I thought this was heavy with symbolism, until Diane told me that dying people sometimes will try to eat whatever is put in front of their face.

Puerto Vallarta

February. The tourist industry in Puerto Vallarta has renamed the downtown beach that runs between La Zona Romantica and El Centro "La Playa del Sol," but to the locals, as also to the t-shirt vendors, it remains La Playa de los Muertos. After three flights to get here, Diane and I sit in lounge chairs talking about our friend Pascale Chow. We have a close-on view of the tourist trade. Pascale is Belgian but met her husband Karl, who brought her to Oxford many years ago, in a place equally tropical—Hawaii. As we try to relax, vendors with shrimp and papaya and langoustines and melon come by every few minutes, making their way around beach towels and chairs and the pasty, middle-aged American crowd. Other vendors polish their jewelry and open their cases: "No, gracias." Sketch artists, tattoo artists, sellers of blankets and indigenous kitsch of all varieties. There's the pier where ten or twelve small boats are moored. One reads "Chico's Dive Shop," another pulls groups of life-jacketed tourists in a rubber canoe, a third tugs the long line that supports the parachute that flies crazy fuckers who want to go up in the sky to look down on Banderas Bay. Under the umbrellas at the tables back toward the hotels, tourists sip beers and margaritas. The men in their tiny speedos make Diane laugh. The better-looking men are down past the pier on the blue chairs under blue umbrellas—the gay area of the beach. We walk through it to climb over rocks at the south end of the beach and find a secluded area

135

where swimming is more difficult. We pass a host of musicians—accordions, guitars, a harp even, on the beach. We've come to get away from the cold, for sun and food and drink. But none of that matters very much because we know that Pascale, Diane's best friend, is dying. For years she's been fighting cancer, and she's near the end. On the first Monday in Mexico we have news at the internet café—she's been taken to a hospice in Hamilton. Three weeks ago she'd been walking her dogs with Diane and Milo. Diane mentions one conversation she had with Pascale after her doctor told her it was time to stop the chemo: "There is no hope." On the beach we have little to do but worry about her. I tell Diane that she'll have a chance to see her again and to help her through her last days, trying not to feel guilty about eating and drinking in a light breeze in the shade of the palapa. Wandering the town one afternoon, we come upon a small cathedral and, inside, witness what we realize is communion on what we suddenly remember is Ash Wednesday. The locals are lined up in the center aisle to approach the altar. We stand in a corner and watch a Mexican man dressed in white moving forward on his knees as the liturgy is intoned. Pascale is already dead.

As for the use of literature in understanding life or making life decisions, I'll settle for what little bubbles up from Robert Walser's prose dribbles as those leak out of genre, even in translation: "I am a little worn out, raddled, squashed, downtrodden, shot full of holes. Mortars have mortared me to bits. I am a little crumbly, decaying, yes, yes. I am sinking and drying up a little. I am a bit scalded and scorched, yes, yes. That's what it does to you. That's life. I am not old, not in the least, certainly I am not eighty, by no means, but I am not sixteen anymore either. Quite definitely I am a bit old and used up. That's what it does to you." In Walser's stories, these short shorts, these "sketches, soliloquies, improvisations, arabesques, and capriccios," as Christopher Middleton calls them, the narrator abides an actively hostile world with wit and stoicism, "a playful serenity behind which hide existential fears" as Wikipedia has it. A landlady knocks, the noise hurting his head. He asks her why she knocks. "You are pretentious," she says, but for no reason, as if even to breathe, much less to think, would leave one vulnerable to *that* accusation. I'm a sucker for that kind of thing. It's like the narrator in one of my favorite stories by Brecht. He decides to go for a walk and, as he reaches the town square, takes one look around and decides to go home immediately and close all the windows. There's no reason given. Perhaps he spots a pigeon he doesn't like—I can't remember the story. Or there's the character in the short short by James Kelman who sees his son fall into a vat of molten metal in a factory and says "Sorry, Huey" while using a long pole to push the son's head, all that's left of him, under the liquid fire. If the father in the Kelman story had said "Sorry, Robert" instead of "Sorry, Huey" it wouldn't be funny. That's a comment about literary *technique*, about how names matter, etc. Here's one about anecdotes: you don't *need* them, to read Walser or anybody else. But you might find them interesting. Walser seems to have "heard voices" as a schizophrenic (lately the diagnosis seems to be Asperger's syndrome). That explains all of the years in the sanatorium, but does it explain the writing in pencil, the endless letters not more than a millimeter high? Walser, too, liked long walks. One day he had enough of life, whether he knew it or not, and went out for a walk and fell dead along the footpath. Use that to make sense of his writing if you think you can. Or read Eudora Welty.

Musharraf, clobbered in elections, hangs on; Castro steps aside for his brother. It looks like it's McCain and Obama, but with primaries in Texas and Ohio ahead somebody circulates a Somali Obama, Obama in a headdress. The headdress signifies nothing, or so says the Somali expert at the BBC. Just about perfect for the politics of fear. Kunstler at *Clusterfuck Nation* says it's a depression, not a recession. Paul Craig Roberts says we'd better read Ralph Gomery on trade, and watch out for false flag operations. "Kosovo and the Empire Crazies" is a nice title. Fifth day of ice crust: it's bad for a dog's pads, Kim Medley says. Bulls trade Ben Wallace to begin youth movement, lose two of three. 40 dead on their way to Karbala. Harassed Afghan farmers move their crop from poppies to cannabis. Paul Krugman off today. *No Country for Old Men* is the winner.

More Callers

First daffodils, first sprigs of green on the thinner branches, as Milo and I walk along the river, its shore turned over and partly collapsed, heaps of sand come up out of the river after a storm, the trail intact but redirected by hikers to skirt a tree downed across it and the danger of this newly proximate, steep riverbank. A week of five poets, including Carla Harryman, Brenda Iijima, and Tyrone Williams. Harryman reads from her book of improvised quatrains entitled *Open Box*, improvised in this case meaning unrevised, the poems written, she says, while she listened to instrumental music and tried to come to grips with the futility of her opposition, everyone's opposition, to the war in Iraq. I liked these little poems when I saw them online as flash files. Little boxes opened to reveal the poem's lines one at a time. But I find that in bunches—she reads the whole book—I like them less. Some of the stanzas are a little prosaic, the lines flat. At other moments the writing is smart and witty:

A score without objective
Open hands deploy
Hope without hope
As future etch

Between a word and a thing
Lives a little dummy

Hired
To make sense of people

The first of these two stanzas (which together make up page 45) seems to describe Harryman's process of composition, and the word "etch" in the fourth line is interesting for the way it suggests that writing is not inscription but something more tentative, not the chiseling on stone of Basil Bunting's *Briggflatts* but more like messing with the knobs on Etch A Sketch. I remain invested in precision, which exists uneasily with improvisation and the "open." The second stanza is funny, though the verb "hired" suggests possibilities that aren't developed. After Harryman read for an hour and fifteen minutes, befuddled students began zipping up their backpacks; this was a little more poetry than they wanted.

Iijima, like Harryman, thinks of herself as a political poet; her politics are a form of eco-politics. Her ear is sharp, circling words in dense sound patterns to push the poems along with the associations sound and rhyme allow, meanwhile presenting critique that folds in the pre-history of Andrei Leroi-Gourhan to trash a modernity totaled by plastic. It is fierce work and more interesting to *hear* than Harryman's because of its sound values. Tyrone Williams is an old friend who has read on campus many times, and it is a delight to hear a little of his new book, *On Spec*, which, like *c.c.* before it, is remarkable for the range of hybrid forms it invents in order to transmute cultural poetics into lyric, to paraphrase the book's blurb, written by Marjorie Welish. I like the little poems in the earlier book, too, since they are intellectually fast:

Tag

Hung up by, on, or
both. Ordinary fruit. Boots
pulled up by, only.

This is from a series of poems in *c.c.* called "Tag" and
alluding to the "tagging" of graffiti artists. And of
course to "Strange Fruit" and the history of lynching
in the United States, and to the Booker T. Washing-
ton work ethic of pulling oneself up by one's boot-
straps.

Limp dicks and ducktails, I think, as Diane and I stand
in a corner of the concourse at the US Bank Arena
in Cincinnati and watch the crowd arrive for Bruce
Springsteen's concert. We spot one man, I want to
call him a "dude," with his hair slicked back like a
greaser though he's pushing 65, wearing pointy boots
and leather pants and a t-shirt that might have looked
good tight on him twenty years ago. He isn't the
worst of it. The fat, the ugly, the evidently stoned—
"the pure products" of Kentucky, as William Carlos
Williams has it—are out in full force for this show,
occasionally with children or grandchildren pulling
behind them. I know that a big part of the appeal of
Springsteen is his ability to speak to or identify with
what used to be called the working class, but if this is
the working class we are in deep shit. The future of
rock n' roll woke up one morning and found that an
army of belching trolls was trailing him. None of this
would bother me if Springsteen let his band play, but
much of his set is canned, the power rock of a fading
generation throwing its fist in the air while attempting
to "rise on up" one more time. Nevertheless, in some

ways, Springsteen himself is a miracle. He looks every
bit as fit as when I last saw him in 1975 in Cleveland,
and still charges around the stage—maybe not quite
so much as he did all those years ago, jumping on
fewer amplifiers, sliding on his knees less. He sings
his lungs out in his husky baritone for hours on end.
The crowd goes nuts pretty much throughout. One
kid three rows in front of us stands up for the entire
show, shaking his fist in circles, as if he were an angry
worker listening to a speech in a bad black and white
movie from the 1930s. It is too easy to make fun
of these people who imagine they can "spit in the
face of these badlands," even if parts of the spectacle
are indeed depressing—Springsteen allowing five or
seven people pushing up against the stage to strum his
guitar as their stroking is projected on giant screens
hanging on each side of the stage, the guitar as enor-
mous prick. I could talk about Philip Auslander's fine
work on "liveness," about the mediated effects of
this and other supposedly "live" experiences in rock
n' roll, but what's the point? Paul Revere and the
Raiders cut to the essence of the problem years ago:
Kicks really are harder to find these days. The pas-
sions that Springsteen sings about are real, though,
and for most fans at the concert not the farce I see.
Their anger is finally anger about their powerlessness.
Springsteen's commitment to musical traditions out
of Woody Guthrie and Pete Seeger and Bob Dylan
is authentic, though for me his best songwriting took
place long ago with his first two albums. He's no
Dylan in performance—really only his version of
"Lost in the Flood" shows an effort to reinvent his
catalog—but he doesn't have to be, doesn't have to
bear that burden of artist or poet. He can belt out
pop songs and folk songs and songs in between and

say, as we hear him say, "Are you having fun yet?"
It's true his mug is up there on the big screen. By
contrast we are offered only the fingers and fretboard
of poor Nils Lofgren, as if he has no body or face
worth seeing blown up big, and the bass player is
still more invisible. Old sidekicks Stevie, Max, and
Clarence get a little more face time in this carefully
ranked cult of personality. But it's pleasant to see that
Springsteen *is* obviously having fun and doesn't take
himself too seriously, even as he presents his canned
political speeches. He's a millionaire many times over,
but he's still the guy playing power chords in a bar.
No wonder the masses like him. My favorite moment
of the show comes when he pulls a young girl up on
stage to shimmy and shake beside him to the chords
of "Dancing in the Dark." I learn later that her name
is Hannah, and that she also performed her Courtney
Cox imitation in Indianapolis two nights earlier. It
seemed so spontaneous.

Bear Stearns bailout unprecedented, the most radical
Fed action since the Great Depression, already fading
in the news cycle: Nouriel Roubini has us in the
swamp for two years, housing not to bottom until
2011 or 2012. New Pakistani government says the old
deal with the US is over. Carla Bruni does a Jackie
O for the British. McCain is out of touch on the
economy and ahead in the polls. Madonna says leave
Britney alone.

Daybook

Bright sun, low wind. Greenery going strong, the crabgrass ahead of better grass. Milo and I walk the far end of the lake, along a sculpted top to the other side, where the spill-off runs into the river. To the right, down the bank, there's a tiny river of red, an iron puddle of uncontained seepage. We walk down the hill around to the point where the spill-off meets the river and, at the end of a short path, are surprised to find two fishermen where we'd never seen fishermen in the fall. One of them is Japanese American, wearing a hoodie and carrying his bucket and pole. He's friendly: "He like to swim?" He likes to wade and drink. The second is an old man yards out in the confluence sitting on his bucket on a slab of concrete. He pays no attention. Meanwhile I'm remembering the photo on Tom Raworth's Flickr site yesterday. It's of a monument to a dog, in Cambridge. Raworth has mentioned the monument before, but today I can read its inscription: "1934. In Memory of Tony A Dog Who Gave Him Friendship And Happiness During His Cambridge Years This Trough Is Erected By His Royal Highness Prince Chula Of Siam." It must be "trough," though it looks like "trouch." There is and will be no monument for Milo, unless it's this book.

Cathy Wagner has a recent chapbook called *everyone in the room is a representative of the world at large*, the

title also naming every poem in the sequence. There
is one poem in the sequence that I especially admire:

> God knows questions are beside the point.
> God understands that it is uncomfortable on top
> of the point.
> God knows that questions help to demarcate the area
> in which the point rises
> leaving it in relief.
> God knows the point rises from its own background
> like a bas-relief, so that if one located it
> one could chisel the whole thing off the
> wall and throw it away.
>
> God help me locate the main melody or rhythm
> of the crickets.
>
> God damn me to six feet of darkness
> between me and the ceiling, what's the point of it?
>
> God grant it.
>
> God grant god knows everything outside the shell
> and nothing
> in, nothing of us. God grant we hatch.
>
> I have
>
> I have a whole world
> to promote★

The poem is fascinating for the way its move-

★ Wagner's *My New Job* (Fence, 2009) includes a different version of
the poem.

ment results from, at one and the same time, simple wordplay and sophisticated, even quasi-philosophical thought. I refer especially to the punning upon and development of the phrase "beside the point." Wagner might well have—might as well have—Wittgenstein and others like John Searle in mind with her line about the point rising "from its own background." The point—er, the claim—of that line is that "the point" (the proposition) is intelligible only as embedded in system, in a form of life, in the ordinary if not always articulated background against which phenomena (and "points") show up as such. Obviously, Wagner's poem also employs the rhetoric of prayer, though its view of the relationship of self to God is not comforting, however hopeful the poem's ending. The speaker wants to break out of the "egg" enclosing us and keeping us unknown by, or apart from, God, but it's from inside that egg that she speaks. As Wittgenstein says in the *Tractatus*, "the sense of the world must lie outside the world."

The circles are very small in so-called advanced poetry, and memory makes them smaller. If the memory is of Charles Bernstein pulling out a cellphone as part of a performance and shouting "Sell! Sell!" into the receiver, it's also of Randolph Healy answering the phone as part of a deadpan improvised talk in Cork: it's his wife calling, wanting to know where he's put something. But the circles are not *that* small—there are just so many poets. Now it's Rodrigo Toscano wishing a group of us a safe trip after breakfast and coffee at the Greenpoint café in Brooklyn the morning after the *Plantarchy* reading Justin Katko organized for us at a SoHo gallery. It's Geraldine Monk making Alan Halsey and Stephen

Rodefer eggs in a student apartment the four of us are sharing at the Victoria Lodge in Cork, an argument with Rodefer the night before now ancient history— or perhaps she wins it this way. It's Rod Smith pulling up in a car with Tom Orange and Mel Nichols and squeezing a plastic frog to greet a group of us outside Peabody Hall on the final morning of the post-moot festival in Oxford. It's post-Fluxus Bill Howe covering a door with butcher paper in Orono, then standing outside the door filming people as they come up to it, waiting to see who will find the nerve to smash through to enter the room for a reading scheduled there—only to find the chairs piled in a corner, a mountain of chairs, so the crowd has to stand up for the reading. One by one they went in. For the life of me I can't remember who broke through.

The last reading of the academic year brings out the biggest crowd. There are colleagues in attendance who haven't been to a poetry reading at the university in many years, if ever, including the dean and an associate provost, administrators and faculty from a range of departments, the usual students as well as the people I expect to see at poetry readings on campus. This is what a Pulitzer Prize does, I guess, or perhaps it is Natasha Trethewey's subject matter that brings them out. She is bi-racial, and many of her poems take up her life story, as does "Mississippi," which remembers that her parents had to leave the state to marry because it was illegal for them to marry in Mississippi. She introduces her reading by noting that she is happy to be in Oxford because of that history— her parents married in Ohio—and reads for forty-five minutes, mostly in the lilting intonations that signify poetry for some poets. I ask the associate provost and somebody else why all of these people have come out, and the answer I get is "publicity," but I know that the publicity for other readings is usually pretty good. Trethewey's poetry is elegiac, despite the anecdotes that frame it, where anger can be glimpsed. And then she really does get a little angry, but at a group of ten or so students who get up to leave about 30 minutes in. She stops several lines into a poem to announce that she will wait for the students to leave, and then when she resumes reading her voice has changed, the lilt is gone, and it's as if we have switched stations and left the easy listening behind. Now I'm really paying attention, no longer condescending to what I take to be poems that don't much interest me, and then she reads a poem about the Gulf Coast after Katrina. "I am the Gulf Coast," the poem says, or I think I hear that it says that. Oh, I think, it's the bard.

Junk

Six weeks of cleaning house, scraping and painting and scrubbing, trashing old junk and giving old furniture away via the local Freecycle Yahoo group. A waterbed left in the garage by a former graduate student, a vinyl recliner. Two salmon-pink living room chairs destroyed by cats. An antique roll-top desk painted peacock blue but without its roll-top attached; we'll never refinish it now. A black vinyl chair and footstool, an antique love seat with one leg broken, Grandfather Tuma's brass lamp, dead de-humidifiers, dead microwaves. Dead computers and dead televisions require a drive to Hamilton for recycling. Democrats continue their mud wrestling, others their aggressive talk about Iran. After a hot start, the Cubs cool off and drop four of five. South Korea clones drug-sniffing dogs. Commodity inflation, food riots, gas at $3.65 and headed up. Sick sex in a secret basement in Austria, sick sex in Texas. Too many write-downs to write up, airlines merge. I mow the yard but leave the creeping charley for its purple flowers.

Anecdotes don't go out of style, but collections of anecdotes do. One of the reasons that collections of anecdotes in the late eighteenth and nineteenth century might have given way is the rise of the novel, the popularity of which must have helped supplant the old-style book of anecdotes. Anecdotes tend to present superficial accounts of purportedly factual events, and to the extent that they depict character they don't bother much with motives or with sketching the logic of action or event. Now we have the more ambitious "memoir." Even a minimally plotted novel or memoir inscribes causality. Then, too, nineteenth-century historiography is all about causality. Goodbye, anecdote—you are now folded in, framed, no longer simply one thing after another, as in Peter Manson's *Adjunct*. And yet of course anecdotes are everywhere. We read about "anecdotal realism" in a book about poetry. Avant-garde poets claim to hate anecdotes or the anecdotal style, though what they really hate is the way that anecdotes are framed. Older forms of history like the chronicle and recent ones like Frank O'Hara's "I did this, I did that" poems allow the anecdote to breathe a little. Anecdotes have no meaning; they have to be given one. Why not leave that business to somebody else, to the reader maybe? We find in the back yard in the bushes a dead cat well along the way in its decomposition. The city won't come out to pick it up, as it isn't in the street. That's the policy. I put it in the trash for Rumpke to pick up, but the stench is bad, so I decide to put it in a box and take it out to the park and put it in a dumpster. It's not *As I Lay Dying*.

Food riots again. Up to half a million dead and the junta in Myanmar blocks UN-sponsored relief. Hezbollah overruns West Beirut. Eggheads and African Americans vote for Obama says the Clinton campaign. Code Pink to try witchcraft at Mother's Day anti-war rally in Berkeley. Jenna Bush and Henry Hager to be married at twilight in front of limestone altar and cross, near a man-made lake on the property in Crawford. 200 guests to gather at a remote location for security sweep, transport to the ranch. Final day of spring semester.

The job looms, so I accept the dean's invitation to attend the annual dinner for administrators in the College of Arts and Science. It has been a hard year in the College, and the dean is asking department chairs to come prepared to tell a joke or funny story to lighten the mood at the dinner. Having been on leave, I want a low profile and so try to avoid doing this, but near the end of the dinner a few clowns on the other side of the room begin chanting my name, and I have to go to the podium. I decide I'll paraphrase a story from Thomas Pynchon's *V.*, the story itself a version of Hawthorne's "The Birthmark." I begin by saying that I don't have a joke, unless the fact that I've been on leave is a joke, or the fact that I am to return to work in August as associate dean. Then I tell them that the story I am going to tell them is an American story. I think that's true. It's a story about a boy who is born with everything going for him. This boy doesn't know how lucky he is because he has one problem, or what he takes to be a problem, and obsesses about it—a golden screw where his navel should be. He wants to be rid of this screw very badly indeed. He consults with a number of people, would-be experts, in search of a plan. That's how I remember the story. He learns that the way to be rid of the screw is to travel to a remote land, where he will find a balloon tree, and atop the balloon tree one special balloon containing a magic screwdriver. This screwdriver will remove his golden navel. He's all for that. He makes the trip and finds the tree, climbs up, pops the balloon, and grabs the magic screwdriver. Then he clambers down, ready for action. One turn of the screw. Two. A third. He feels it happening, the screw coming out at last. Then it's out. Then his ass falls off. The story goes something like that, and that's something like I tell it, walking away from the podium after the punch line. The audience of my peers is not quite sure what to make of the story. Then the dean stands up and tells a better one. It's about the professor who wants an appointment with the dean and learns he can't have one because the dean has died. He comes back anyway and asks again, then a third time. The dean's secretary finally says, "How many times do I have to tell you? The dean can't meet with you. The dean is dead!" The professor says, "I know. I just wanted to hear you say it one more time."

What matters most to me about scholarship is the pleasure that attends the discovery of something unexpected. And some of the scholars I admire most are the ones who pursue scholarship for pleasure, outside of the university, independent scholars. Andrew Duncan is one, however much I disagree with his polemics concerning recent British poetry. But it is Nate Dorward who best defines the species for me. We worked together on *Anthology of Twentieth-Century British and Irish Poetry*, and, if that book is at all useful, Dorward's annotations are a big part of that. Dorward might have been a professor, but he never really wanted the job, I think. I have heard him say that he doesn't think he would enjoy standing up in front of people to teach them, which is a silly notion, as I have watched him talk on his feet quite nimbly. Not that he has always been nimble in a literal sense, I must say. I have a memory of him leaping a puddle in the streets of Cork a little less than gracefully. He is a large man, or he was then; these days he is much thinner. Dorward's leap might have happened the same year a group of us, Karen Mac Cormack and cris cheek and Drew Milne and Dorward, discovered a man swimming for his life in the River Lee. We were walking around the city after the festival was over. There's no easy way out of the river, since the steps leading up the concrete walls on both sides of the river are some distance apart. Karen and cris hollered until the fire department arrived to toss the swimmer a line. Others were hollering too. Karen remembers this in her remarkable book *Implexures*, which features a kind of anecdotal writing more experimental than what you find in this book. I'm remembering the event because I'm also remembering that Dorward has often rescued me when I needed information and feedback about my writing. Sometimes I think there is nothing he doesn't know at least a little about; he is certainly the best editor I know. More important than his talent, though, is his generosity, his willingness to photocopy for pretty much anybody who wants it a rare pamphlet of small press poetry, to send it to them gratis. That's the spirit I associate with the world of small press poetry, the world I have been remembering here, and with the energy that is outside the profession of literary study and the profession of creative writing, outside the business of writing and getting published, the prizes and elite discourse.

Elbert Hubbard was one of the most prolific authors in American literature, a key figure in the American Arts and Crafts movement. Editor of *The Philistine*, friend of Carl Sandburg, novelist and popular lecturer, much quoted in his day, Hubbard (1856–1915) is perhaps best remembered for his *Little Journeys* series, and for dying on the Lusitania. Modeled after

Plutarch's *Lives of the Noble Greeks* and *Lives of the Noble Romans*, Hubbard's *Little Journeys* appeared monthly for fourteen years. An advertisement in one of the *Little Journeys* published by Hubbard's Roycroft Publications in 1902 lists the circulation for the series at 60,000, much larger than the circulation of most poetry magazines today. The *Little Journeys* were sometimes used as textbooks, and they still have their fans, as one website demonstrates: "Elbert Hubbard is dead, or should we say, has gone on his last Little Journey to the Great Beyond. But the children of his fertile brain still live and will continue to live and keep fresh the memory of their illustrious forebear." Each *Little Journey* offers a brief life of an eminent artist, writer, musician, or statesman, complete with life-improving advice; each also includes a description of the home of the person whose life is briefly told. The little books have their share of anecdotes, which thrive in this kind of work mixing travel writing, biography, and art criticism. I have the idea that they might be imitated.

From Orono
to Yellow Springs

It's early morning the day after the death of NBC newsman Tim Russert is in the news, and Barrett Watten greets me beside the bagels in the break-fast room of the Orono University Inn, wondering what I think about this news. I'm not thinking much about it so I ask him what *he* thinks. "You know, do away with the ripples." Russert was thought by some to be the television journalist most skeptical of the administration's claims. "I'm not much for conspir-acy theories," I reply. I think of other times over the years when Watten has made similar remarks about the state of the world. It's a form of greeting, not meant altogether seriously, one of Watten's ways of being friendly. Earlier in the conference Watten gave a paper about language poetry and late capitalism and argued that those who want to write the movement's history must credit its political motivations and not read it exclusively through formalist lenses, as one more chapter in the history of the revolution of the word. In Orono the 1970s turn out to have been all about the language poets. It's not cynical to say that the group's writing about poetry and politics seems like ancient history now, academic, small talk like the breakfast greeting. In saying that, I don't want to deny the value of Watten's work as critic and poet, or to surrender to hopelessness. "Cynicism is the playground of the middle class," Baraka said to me when he visited Oxford, and there is nothing cynical about either Baraka or Watten—they are earnest in the extreme, albeit in different ways.

The following morning in the same ratty breakfast nook I have a brief conversation with Bob Perelman and Rae Armantrout in which Perelman admits that he finds the prospect of Obama being elected after eight years of Bush cause for hope, as Obama will present a new face of America to the world. I mention what I've heard about the money coming into Obama's campaign from Wall Street and the possibility that the people doing long-term geo-strategic planning will only shuffle desks, but Perelman isn't having any of it.

The black bear in the lobby at the University Inn is stood up beside a potted plant. Breakfast downstairs happens next to a room with a pool table, mirrors with stenciled beer labels, and an old-style big-screen television, as in a suburban rec room. The motel, probably dating from the 1960s, is clean but worn, paint peeling from the cinderblock walls framing the patios outside each room's sliding door. Most of the action is at the pool around back, college kids soaking up beer and sun, ignorant of the conference. Diane joins them in the afternoon, taking a pass on the papers. I've been thinking that the conference will be a gold mine of anecdotes, but I find myself struck by how many of the people I remember from past Orono conferences aren't at this one. Some of them are dead, including two of Maine's own, Sylvester Pollet and Burt Hatlen. Hatlen I saw at the Pound conference in Venice a year ago. We sat by the water and talked, waiting for the vaporetto to come around to San Servolo. He'd been fighting cancer for years, but that day he was worried about his big toe, which he'd banged against something, and wondering if he ought to see an Italian doctor. With Carroll Terrell, Hatlen built an institution that has furthered the study of poetry, and he did it in a self-effacing manner and at some cost to his own career as scholar and poet. I'm missing also Peter Quartermain, whose sharp close readings of poetry in the Pound tradition always make me feel a little stupid, and Alan Golding and Norman Finkelstein and many others I associate with the conference. At the same time, the poets featured at the conference are mostly the same poets who have been through Oxford over the last few years. It's good to see them, but there's also the feeling of running in place. Rae Armantrout is a featured reader, and we talk in the hallway outside one venue. She says she's been telling people about our trip to the museum. Bernadette Mayer is here too. We chat in the lobby outside the Colby College Art Museum, where the conference moves for an afternoon to see paintings by Alex Katz and Joe Brainard and for her reading and Clark Coolidge's. Bernadette has recently tumbled down a hillside so has her arm in a plastic cast and a broken bone in her neck, but she's all smiles, wearing the same hat she wore in Oxford. Clark Coolidge walks up as we're talking, and Bernadette turns to greet him, "Hello, Clark, how's your masculinity?" I don't catch his answer but can tell he's used to Bernadette's remarks. He's wearing one of the Hawaiian shirts he's been wearing all week, with a silk jacket; he's easy-going and quiet, and I find I like him. When Bernadette asks him to come up and read part of something they wrote together long ago, he does so reluctantly, and then he reads from his own work in a deep voice, emphasizing its deadpan wit. He's been around long enough to roll his eyes at all of this. Before Bernadette reads, she says, sitting in a chair beside the podium, "Poetry or penis size: does either really matter?"

For four days it's a party, papers and readings, the late-night open mike. Diane and I spend time with Justin Katko and his young friends Ryan Dobran and Michael Sokolowski. On the last night, Katko and I read part of our collaborative poem *Holiday in Tikrit*. During Kevin Killian's performance, the cameraman, Jimmy Shorter, had been on stage with him, circling Killian with his camera, so when it's our turn I jump out of the frame every time he points the camera my way. Meanwhile, the other world—I'd call it the "real world" but in many ways it's more "unreal" even than this conference world—is never far away. We see it at the Bangor airport as we're waiting for the flight and notice that the airport is beginning to fill up with Marines in their desert uniforms. I overhear a few of them talking and discover they are headed for Iraq, via Shannon and a base in Germany. As we wait in the bar inside, we sit at the table in a corner near two African American soldiers and one Hispanic soldier and watch old footage of George W. Bush trying to dance beside a few Africans in traditional dress. We go through security and wait inside acrylic walls, turning to watch the soldiers, hundreds of them, walking in single file up to a special gate behind us. Old men and women wearing Lion's Club hats wait to shake their hands as they board the jet.

Because we've been in Bar Harbor and Orono, we miss a family reunion in Thornville, Ohio occa-

sioned by the return of my Singapore-based cousin
Brad Blackstone and his wife and daughter. They
return annually to visit my aunt and cousins, and I
have many pleasant memories of spending time with
them. Apart from Diane and Allison, my father and
sisters and their families, the people in Thornville and
nearby Pleasantville are the family I know—my uncle
and his kids are in Australia or England. In recent
years, going up to Thornville has also meant the
chance to play music with Brad and his wife, Karen
Nunis Blackstone, who has released two CDs of her
songs. I stop in Columbus on the way and pick up my
friends Aaren Yandrich and Leah Wahlin, so they can
bring their instruments along to the party. I'm in no
hurry on the way home the following afternoon, so
stop for a bite to eat in Yellow Springs. The college
there, Antioch, has closed, but the town is enjoying
the return of its alumni anyway, so I take a pass on a
crowded old pub that claims to be one of the oldest in
Ohio and duck into a Subway instead. Then it's over
to the used bookstore down the street to check out
the poetry section. No book there tempts me, though
I glance at a translation of Tasso. As I'm scanning the
shelves to the right of the poetry section, my eye lands
on the green dust jacket of Clifton Fadiman's collection of anecdotes, *The Little Brown Book of Anecdotes*.
I've had the library's copy, but I can't resist, since
the bookstore wants only eight bucks for it. I flip the
book over and read the text on the jacket, which I
hadn't seen on the library's copy:

YOU WILL DISCOVER THESE BIO-
GRAPHICAL INCIDENTS:

Why Augustus despaired of his daughter Julia

How Charlemagne invented white wine
Why Hideyoshi gave up on Buddha
What Clara Barton distinctly remembered to
  forget
Why John Rockefeller never got his nickel back
  from a pay phone
What King Faisal wore under his robes

YOU WILL FIND THEM INTERESTING:

What Ferenc Molnár said when he saw his first
  rush hour

AND AMUSING:

What happened at a performance of George
  Antheil's Ballet mécanique

MOVING:

Charles de Gaulle's observation on the death of
  his daughter

USEFUL:

How Sir Herbert Beerbohm Tree introduced
  two friends whose names had escaped him

RIDICULOUS:

Yogi Berra's reaction to a check made out to
  "Bearer"

AND EVEN RIBALD:

Calvin Coolidge's interest in the mating habits
   of roosters

I can't compete with that. In Orono, I was trying to
explain my book to Lytle Shaw and Patrick Pritchett,
so I'm pleased when Patrick emails me a few days
after my return from Thornville to tell me he's found
a passage in Walter Benjamin's *The Arcades Project* that
might interest me: "The constructions of History are
comparable to the institutions of the military, which
browbeat daily life and assign it to barracks. Over
against that, the anecdotal is like a street fight or an
insurrection." That takes me back to Joel Fineman
and the New Historicism.

I take Milo over to walk on campus by Peabody and
Boyd, but it's hot and humid and he doesn't want to
walk much. We settle for a trip around Boyd, peeking
through the mesh fence to look at the digging going
on for the university steam tunnel. Then back
through the brick center of town to see that tents are
up and a jazz band playing in the square. I figure I'll
take Milo home and come back to see what's going
on. It turns out to be a wine tasting and local artists
festival, sponsored by the Chamber of Commerce.
Jean Vance tells me this in front of her watercolors,
priced at 25, 50, and 100 dollars—I'm surprised she's
the only person I recognize. She tells me about the
Oxford Community Arts Center, where cris cheek
and I used to rent a studio. There's an elevator now,
she says. This Center is a worthwhile project, the
building an old women's dormitory donated by the
university. An Eagle Scout has renovated the library,
Jean tells me. My friend Billy Simms has a studio
there—he's a high school teacher for his day job. So

does John Kogge, who's been playing covers of folk and folk-rock forever and runs a frame shop in town. cris and I didn't have much use for the studio so gave it up after putting on an event where we filmed ourselves picking at a hole in the plaster, and another group performance where cris read a long piece offering his thoughts about community as an Englishman in his new home. It was a lot of fun, if pretty odd to the locals. A classics professor I have known for years came up to me afterwards and asked, "Who *are* these people?" It ended with Bill and Lisa Howe singing the Police song about the fate of the dinosaurs, "Walking in Your Footsteps," while wearing plastic bags over their heads. At the wine tasting I don't want to pay the twelve dollars for four small samples so grab a sandwich across the street and turn to go home. I don't look at the art in the square but walk past Kona Restaurant and see that one artist has work there, his exhibit sponsored by Duke Energy. It turns out to be landscapes by one of my department chair colleagues, oil paintings titled *Duck Creek on Wood* or something like that. I walk by without going in and head a few blocks down the street to the Community Center to have a look at the Experimental Children's Garden that is on its grounds. Its flowers and ironwork are simple but well-maintained, stones between flowerbeds, a picnic table in the middle of the garden. Perhaps the garden is a little crowded, I think, the inner art snob emerging. The market is down 20% since October. The Saudis say they'll pump a little more oil but we'd better get used to oil prices rising. All down the Mississippi they're cleaning up from the floods. The Cubs are hanging on in first and the Bulls have drafted Derrick Rose with the first pick in the 2008 NBA Draft.

Diane reads my sentences about the Orono conference and says, "I know you think you have to
write about these so-called famous people, but it's
the other stuff I find more interesting." She means
the people we ran into in Bar Harbor and Blue Hill
before the conference, and in Bangor the morning
we blew off the conference for breakfast there. She
means the woman at the gallery in Bar Harbor who
explained why sea glass is more expensive in certain
colors—"You find more beer bottles than these old
milk of magnesia bottles these days." She means the
woman with her dog in a small city park. Or Megan,
the young woman from Arizona working in the
gift shop on top of Cadillac Mountain. We ask her
about a photo shoot happening in the mist. He's an
actor, she says, what's his name? But I ask the photographer during a break, and it turns out he's only a
male model; they're shooting an ad for a New York
department store. "So he's just a model," I say to
the photographer. "Not just any model." She means
Larry and Scott and Scott's dog Splash in a little restaurant in Blue Hill. We sit next to these three, and
Scott immediately strikes up a conversation with
Diane, thinking she's somebody else. Diane introduces us and shakes Scott's hand—he's blind, and he
has a panic disorder, he tells us. Splash is well trained
but Scott doesn't know how he stands it in Maine
since he's a dog from the tropics. Larry is older, with
the beard and body of a man who might work his
Christmas holidays as Santa. He's obviously very kind.
They leave before Diane's lobster and my lobster roll
arrive. As we sit in the diner, I misquote a line from
Robert Lowell's *Life Studies* about the red fox stain on
Blue Hill. The poetry of the personal anecdote run
through the Freud machine.

And life has a way of taking over; we know that much. As these anecdotes sink into memoir, I'm more narcissistic than ever. The impossibly kind Patrick Pritchett writes again and tells me he found the Benjamin quote in a footnote by Fred Jameson. The anecdote book is a good idea, he says again: "Poets seem to thrive on gossip; the wonder is that no one has yet had the wit to see how central this is to literary economy and a sense of community." I'm not sure that this is true or that I have gossip to offer, not in a book meant as a tribute to friends and acquaintances, or new information about the economy of poetry—never exactly the "gift economy" it would like to be—or poetry's communities. Should I imagine that I am writing or recording this "gossip" for communities of poets and readers of recent poetry, or only for friends and acquaintances? I lost my way somewhere back there. I'm making it up as I go along. It's not like the anecdote is any one thing.

Diane passes on the trip to Thornville because she wants to recover from a few night shifts and get ready for Relay for Life, where Pascale will be honored in the Luminary Ceremony, her name read out. We head over after dinner to the track between the basketball and football stadiums. It's rained earlier and we spot a rainbow. It might be a little sugary to mention it here, but it's as real as the double rainbow we'd seen in Orono, which a group of us spotted as we walked across a parking lot. At the track, we run into a few people—my predecessor as associate dean, Steve DeLue; Vicky Dynes; my former student Blade Hill and his wife Julie; another former student, Tom Schmidlin, and his wife Jennifer. Tom's playing in a band on center stage as we arrive. Pascale's husband

Karl Chow is there, their son Alexi. We walk around the track where paper bags bearing the names of cancer victims are placed and filled with sand to weigh them down, folded to expose candles inside. The bags are sagging from the rain earlier, and Diane tries to straighten a few of them. Then at twilight the candles are lit and we all walk a memorial lap. Ten or fifteen people line up beside the stage to prepare to read the names. First comes the list of survivors.

Les Anecdotiques

Diane and I want a little more time to ourselves before I return to work, and we won't go to Cork this year, so we decide to head to South Carolina and the beach. We'll make it up as we go, pick places to stop and stay. "Just like kids," Allison says. "Just like old people," says Diane's mother. I write a few friends who have been on my mind of late and ask them to send me a sentence a day—something they've seen, something overheard, an anecdote. Two of them are to be in Cork for the festival, so I'm thinking I might get a taste of that from a distance, and the others—the plan is to open up the narrative to move it beyond navel-gazing. But I learn quickly that not everybody has the same idea about what I'm hoping for, much less about what might count as an anecdote.

We get a late start the day we leave and don't make it as far south as we'd hoped, stopping in Maggie Valley, North Carolina after a long lunch in Berea, Kentucky. Berea is a college town, and on the way to the diner and a goat cheese salad we walk past a bookstore with John Bradford's *Notes on Kentucky* and another book called *Laughter in Appalachia* displayed in the window. An older guy in a goatee and a younger man I think must be his lover sit out front playing chess. Behind the diner, a young man with rasta dreads sits and chats with a woman toying with a banjo. The diner has a stage, we see, and a collection of mirrors hung like paintings on its brick walls. As we eat, I listen to the conversation of one young student and his girlfriend at the next table. She's wearing glasses and a loose hippie chick skirt. He's trying to impress her by talking about the difference between something he's calling "classical theory" and something he's calling "jazz theory." Later he mentions "the Norwegian tenor," and I can see she's trying to act interested. It costs a lot to go to Berea College and be alternative like they are, which has me remembering my year teaching at Reed College long ago. Not much has changed.

The highway is the highway whether it's hills or mountains you're driving through. You have to get off and onto the smaller roads to see anything, like the signs for Mexican restaurants named "Mexican Restaurant" or an odd sign I can't quite decode—"The Swag." It's dusk by the time we pull into Maggie Valley, a town full of bikers. The signs on the hotels and motels read "God Bless Trooper Blanton." I learn from a quick Google search in the room that he was a state trooper murdered some time ago. There are signs for Hot Boiled Pea-nuts, and a club called The Stompin Ground, which advertises Western Carolina's largest dance floor for clogging. Our motel is surrounded by carved black bears. There's a cheap tapestry with an eagle descending upon its prey, another with a large-mouthed bass leaping clear of its stream, a fish out of proportion. I park next to a huge motorcycle, and take care in opening my door—this motorcycle is expensive, I can tell. Its owner greets me—he's an older man from Troy, Ohio, up near Dayton, probably a businessman. He comes every year, he says, to ride the mountain roads. The Maggie Valley Diner is good for breakfast.

On day two, we decide to make up ground and try to get all the way to the water, but we notice that we'll be driving through Flat Rock, North Carolina so decide to stop there to check out the Carl Sandburg home, a national historic site, the first national park dedicated to an American poet. We're thinking that nobody is likely to be interested and we'll have the place to ourselves, but when we pull into the parking lot we see that it's full. I'm remembering Elbert Hubbard and also Brock Clarke's novel *An Arsonist's Guide to Writers' Homes in New England*, which I heard him read from last fall, a darkly comic send-up of heritage culture. It's a beautiful park, with a large pond and working farm, a barn for the goats Sandburg's wife used to keep. The house sits on a hill, and we hike up to it and pay the five bucks for the tour. Four or five couples are part of our group. Before the tour begins, Diane warns me not to say anything sarcastic. I don't say a word but do sign the guestbook: "Nice work if you can get it." The house was built in 1838 by Gustavus Memminger, later the Secretary of the Treasury for the Confederacy. The irony of the great populist poet-singer and Lincoln biographer buying this house is not lost on us, but neither is the beauty of the vista we're introduced to on the porch, mountains blue in the distance. The couples on the tour are talkative. When the guide mentions that Memminger built the house and outlines his role in the Confederacy, one man says, "That's not such a bad thing." When his wife mentions that the house feels masculine in its furnishings, he adds, "That's as it should be." We watch him grab her ass as we walk into Sandburg's wife's bedroom. I try to look at the books on the shelves, but the tour moves quickly, and we are kept on the carpet runners. The books are organized in a way only Sandburg understood. I spot a couple of old *Poetry* magazines sitting on tables and desks and a book on ethnomusicology, a patch of T. S. Eliot, a row of paperback mysteries. Upstairs we walk past one thin shelf where I see that Sandburg owned a copy of Judge Carter's *The Old Court House: Reminiscences and Anecdotes of the Courts and Bar of Cincinnati.* And on a dresser in his wife's bedroom I spot *The Percy Anecdotes.* The tour guide is more interested in discussing old television sets and a few of the paintings. She lingers in the room where Mrs. Sandburg kept her files for the farm. I see that one drawer is labeled "Why Goat Milk?" The content of the tour, unsurprisingly, is primarily anecdotes about the house and the poet and his family. She explains that he collected canes rather than using them, preferring—she cites his remark—to lean on his wife. She shows us where the family played music; Sandburg owned three guitars. There's one open in its case on top of the baby grand, which leads me to wonder if his wife played the piano. There's a *Life* magazine with a drawing or a photograph—it's hard to tell at a glance—of Bobby Kennedy, and an ashtray with cigar stub. The house has been left as it was when Mrs. Sandburg sold it to the park service for 200k, "all she needed," though the guide tells us that she was offered twice that. Like the cigar stub, these anecdotes enhance the authenticity effect the park service seeks, but it's hard to tell if they interest our group. The fact that Sandburg was a poet, and the nature of his poetry, occupy the group as little as the books in nearly every room of his house, even the basement, which served as a summer kitchen— extra shelves were built here, the guide says. Mrs.

Sandburg's expensive Swedish stove, the use of this or that in the basement to warm baby goats in the winter—this is what the guide discusses. I'm curious about all of that, too, though I don't particularly care to hear the answer to one question somebody asks about why the house does not feature photographs of Sandburg at the White House. It occurs to me that the group probably knows nothing of Sandburg's poetry, though I suppose there's a chance they've heard that Chicago is the city of broad shoulders. This is not how poetry is preserved, I think; it is how nation is sanctified. Nobody lives in the house. But it's a nice park, a bright pleasant day in July. The state owns the grounds, but it doesn't own my perspective walking them. We head for the barn to see the goats.

Katko is the first to respond among those I ask to send sentences. He's on his way to Cork, and he's willing to try anything. Four or five emails land before we make it out the door. I have not told the people I have written what I think an anecdote is, and I have told them only a little about what I mean to do with their sentences, and I'm not sure myself about any of that. It occurs to me after I have written them that by setting an arbitrary limit of one sentence a day—asking them to write me about something over-heard or witnessed—I have made it very difficult for my correspondents to present me with anything but decontextualized fragments. With only one sentence to work with, narrative will be difficult, that's certain, even the kind of framing that locates the participant observer or situates an overheard remark. True to form, Katko ignores my instructions and fires off emails with subject headings such as anecdotal, ankle dotal, a neck, a nick, ank, airpoet, ankle spoken, angry nothings, angel doting, and angle nothings. Here are his first five emails:

I was just here thirty minutes ago and since I got back, someone has broken into the basement window and left the front door unlocked. The third floor is a mess you guys!

A special effect wherein the blinds are turned to let in the light, each blind parallel to the ground, and moving head up and down while looking out at the house next door (and specifically the horizontal shadows beneath each slat, parallel to the blinds) creates an illusion of speed, as the slat lines move down with my head, and the blinds kind of stay where they are. Parallax stuff. Fractal drool.

At this point, it's worth noting that my email inbox has 1420 unread messages. By placing the thumb of my left hand straight into the air at the correct location between my head and the screen (effectively signaling a thumbs directly up at the computer), I am able to block out the number 1, thus allowing my inbox message number to read 420. This number has a secret history and I am pleased with my discovery.

Pulling off tight black t-shirt, collar squeezes head and creates a vacuum in my right ear, dull pain as it releases.

It was one of those salads that demanded oral tossing . . .
Yeah, we're moving in; the landlord's a dick.

Katko is moving apartments in Providence. I know
that already so can make sense of some of this. I
can only speculate that somebody—Katko himself
perhaps—has spoken the final fragment recorded
here. I find that I am least sure about what to make
of the first fragment. The experience of the break-in
might or might not be real.

As Katko continues with his emails, I see that uncer-
tainty about what constitutes an anecdote is creeping
into his consciousness:

> I'm seein robots, passin by everyday. I'm seein
> robots.
>
> Holy shit the fog on the hill!
>
> Is it an anecdote yet? How do you turn this
> thing on? How to make it flip yonder anecdotal
> thresh'?

Even now, I'm not sure that there is a threshold a text
has to cross to become an anecdote, or rather in order
to deserve that label, but it would seem to be the
case that the kind of self-consciousness that Katko's
writing exhibits defeats the logic of anecdotal narration. Watching yourself watching, telling a story about
telling a story, isn't something that happens much
with anecdotes. These fragments—about pulling off
a t-shirt, looking at blinds, reading email—suggest
modes of hyper-consciousness, experience staged by
the desire to narrate or analyze it. By contrast anecdote feeds on fact and event, though of course what
is right in front of the nose will depend on whose

nose we're talking about. But the anecdote tends to be naïve about the conditions that shape observation and narration, and about language. Or some of them are. In these brief fragments fired off quickly, Katko seems to be pushing against the anecdotal.

My other correspondents struggle with my request in different ways. Aaren Yandrich is back in Columbus studying for his comprehensive exam. He worries that nothing interesting is happening around him. I tell him that anecdotes don't have to be fascinating, often aren't. But he has mixed up the anecdote with the aphorism for the moment. Some of his sentences:

> It's difficult to be enthusiastic when you know you've got to wait another year before, maybe, something will happen.

> I guess it's good to have a knack.

> Rather than resignation, why not suicide, like in the olden days?

When I download this last one in the hotel, I panic a little—Yandrich is one of my favorite people, and I worry that the push to prep for his exam is getting to him, especially in a job market as hopeless as the market for professors of literature. But it turns out he's thinking about the Bush administration. I think that he's tossing me his sentences without too much thought. One comes accompanied with a footnote:

> Here's a better sentence from Atyana: My good chewing tooth is loose.

Atyana is his daughter, and he's right: it is a better

sentence, and moreover closer to the spirit of some anecdotes. The following day he comes across with something in that same spirit:

> I pretended to play gypsy music on one string.

Yandrich is right to gravitate to the aphorism, given my weak directions: the aphorism better suits the one sentence limit.

In Cincinnati, Steve Lansky, a fiction writer and performance artist who was also once my student and now is a colleague, weighs in with a couple of sentences that offer narrative details that might belong to a story but aren't sufficient by themselves to constitute an anecdote:

> Silver painted toes on black flip-flops walk flip-flip, flip-flip, flip-flip down the hot sidewalk past the café.

> A man wearing a white canvas hat sits in a lawn chair on the sidewalk blocking a short alley next to an alloy easel, sketching passersby for tips.

I'm confident reading these that they derive from what Lansky has seen in his neighborhood in Cincinnati, but they aspire to the artfulness of fiction in a way that most anecdotes don't, particularly that onomatopoeic flip-flop. Well, he *is* a fiction writer.

My cousin Brad in Singapore comes closest to the mark in recounting part of his daily experience, exotic for me because of his location:

At Clementi Station today the bus fumes conjured up memories of another place many years past.

We walked west on Toh Tuck Road a couple blocks to a side street, turned left and saw the tall durian tree, full of spiny fruit.

Singaporeans say that the weather is cloudier this year than any time they can ever remember.

The girls came back from JB with a Ramly burger for me and nasi lemak for themselves.

Self-assured Tamil dudes pull their pants up way high.

Even here, it's clear that one sentence just won't do the trick. So my plan to move the book of anecdotes beyond an increasingly repulsive self-regard fails miserably for lack of good instructions and a firm grasp of what it means to write an anecdote. My bad.

On Folly Beach outside Charleston, the crowd is nearly as white as the sand, though not so white as the people on the beach at the Outer Banks, where we've spent time on the water in years past. The pier is very long; the poetry is nowhere. The hotel is comfortable, with a balcony that opens to the ocean, though it's plenty warm and humid, and if we run the air conditioner it is difficult to distinguish between its hum and the rhythm of the waves. We're happy to be here, as usual when we're near the ocean, and we wander about and eat or sit in the hotel bar and talk about the people we see and the people we know at home and elsewhere. Daniel Ereditario writes from

Cork to tell me that the TSA has no rules about filming. "Boxes come and go; clouds articulate the sky," cris cheek writes from Oxford, his contribution to the anecdote project, referring to the fact that Bill and Lisa Howe have just moved into his house on what must be a sunny day in Oxford. The beach raises testosterone levels in both men and women, I read online. Bush will go to Beijing for the Olympics later in the summer. Exxon and the rest of the major oil companies are officially welcomed back to Iraq.

We have to leave to get north but have breakfast at the hotel, where we overhear a father telling his children at the next table, "I want you all to listen very closely. There are no sharks in the water." We find this pretty funny because the day before we had walked to the far end of the pier, where we watched fishermen pull sharks out of the water. Because there are rules about fishing for sharks, they tossed them back.

After Folly Beach, we head over to Charleston for the Fourth of July. We're in the historic district, it's hot, and there's not much except tourist stuff to do, and we don't feel like doing it. So we wander a bit and find some Italian food, tired of seafood after Maine and Folly Beach. It's impolite to photograph the man passed out on the bricks a block down from the Hibernian Society, so I don't, nor the man I determine is homeless sleeping under a tree in Marion Square. We wander the streets and look in a few shops, check out the graveyards on the grounds of a few churches—Diane tells me that Spanish moss is neither Spanish nor moss.

The last stops on this impromptu and aimless car vacation are Asheville, where we have the best meal of the summer at a Japanese-Thai restaurant, and the Pine Mountain State Resort Park in Pineville, Kentucky, which features indescribably beautiful views of the mountains. In Asheville we find what we expect to find, the third generation backwash of the 1960s. Guitarists on the streets in all shapes and sizes, thick with stink and six month beards, one with a pink headband sitting under a sign flashing a message about the Biltmore Estate, another outside a vegetarian café with a young man on the pavement beside him typing on a laptop. We walk by one with a woman in a wheelchair accompanying him—I join him for the chorus of "Don't Think Twice It's All Right." We've been to Asheville before and like it well enough and talk about how odd it is that Allison has so little use for these cultural styles, which we don't take altogether seriously but find harmless. Diane points out a coffee mug in one shop with a yellow chick on it and the words "hippie chick," and I try to remember the Camper Van Beethoven lyrics we heard on the way to Folly Beach, something about being willing to die for hippie chicks but wanting to stop to skate a bit first. The Cork festival is much on our mind, though it is thousands of miles away, and in honor of Trevor Joyce and our friends in Cork we stop to have a drink at an Irish pub. First it was the Hibernian Society in Charleston, headquarters for the Stephen A. Douglas faction in the election of 1860, proudly displaying its section of the Giant's Causeway. Now it's the pub.

While Asheville is an obvious stop, Pine Mountain is not. We'd thought to stay near Cumberland Gap, but neither the park nor the surrounding area there do much for us. An antique shop in the tiny town of Cumberland Gap, Tennessee, however, brings a surprise. The so-called antiques are junk to us, but upstairs the owner has a few books, including five hardbound copies of Terry Eagleton's *After Theory*, and I buy a copy. I look at it a little in the room at the Pine Mountain State Resort and see that 9/11 figures importantly in it, and that it includes a predictable anti-American rant. The lodge is nearly deserted, which makes the views all the more outstanding. Among the few people eating in the restaurant, there's a table of seven or eight men, two of them wearing the same peacock-blue t-shirt, "plugged into god" its text, a light bulb for the "o" in "God." This is God's country, then; maybe that's why the park is deserted. As we wait to pay, I see that one man remains at the table, his eyes closed in prayer. We decide to stay an extra day, it's that peaceful; we want to hike out to the famous Chained Rock. It turns out there's nothing threatening about the rock, which is part of the mountain but appears to loom above the town of Pineville in the valley below. Legends about it are as ripe as Dr. Seuss's Grinch, and daredevil exploits have followed, Herculean labor involving mules and men hauling the huge chain up the mountain to pound it into rocks.

All in the Family

All in the family: IndyMac, Freddie Mac, and Fannie Mae. Wachovia. The blogosphere learns the meaning of "moral hazard," "agency debt." Extra innings for the All Star Game. Spain, Ireland, Germany, Britain: "hard landings" for all. China and Russia with half a trillion of Fannie and Freddie; the sovereign wealth fund solution doesn't look so good this time around. Afghanistan again. Madonna to divorce; Obama to Middle East and Europe. Cubs two and a half up.

We decide to go up to the Akron–Cleveland area to see family, via Ann Arbor to have a look at the art fair. There are hundreds of booths, as they probably call them, rows and rows of white tents throughout the downtown area. We don't see much that we want to look at, apart from the crowd, though we stop to chat with a woman working at the tent for *The Spark*, the Detroit-based socialist newspaper. I buy a copy and ask her how socialism is doing in Detroit. Not so well, she says, but she's hopeful things are looking up with the hard times in the auto industry. Her tent is among a row of tents for religious organizations, most of them Christian, though the organizers have put hers next to one for an Islamic organization. Down the block a bit, as we tire of the art and begin photographing graffiti and looking for a place to eat, we find an alley that's colorful and photograph a skate-boarder having fun in it. There's also a young man sitting at the end of the alley with a sign and loose coins; he asks us to photograph him and email the photograph to him. Diane asks him for his name and address. It's Hollywood, he says, though his Yahoo address suggests something else. He's an artist; he wants photographs to put up on his MySpace page. I've had luck with the bookstores in Ann Arbor, so we walk over to Shaman Drum, but it's about to close and I don't see anything. Then it's around the corner and down the block to Dawn Treader, a used book-store I've always liked. In the poetry section, I see what I take to be the same Clayton Eshleman books I saw on these shelves several years ago, the last time I was in Ann Arbor. It's obviously the owner who is working the register, so I ask him about that—he must know Eshleman, who lives only a few miles away, in Ypsilanti. He's a good poet, the owner says, but his books don't sell. He asks me if I've been to his house. "He must have a million dollars of paintings in that house," I say, exaggerating for effect. He nods. "Buy some art," he says, "if you find any."

Before we check into the hotel off the highway between Cleveland and Akron, in Stow, Ohio, we stop to buy flowers for my mother's gravesite—this will be the first time I've seen the stone my father ordered. The grass is thin at the site, and that and the earth caving in one row over means I must try to avoid imagining my mother's body in her coffin six feet below. The stone is impressive, the big letters TUMA up top and my mother's name and dates in a smaller font below on the right, my father's name and birthdate to the left. I see that he has asked that an icon representing the Bible be carved in the marble, a small rectangle with a cross and the letters KJV, my father's preferred translation—he is adamant about it. Citations for, but not the text of, verses from the Bible are above each name, Revelation 21.1–21.21 for my mother, John 14.1–17.25 for my father. A new heaven and a new earth, all the tears wiped away: "And he that sat upon the throne said, Behold, I make all things new. And he said unto me, Write: for these words are true and faithful." From the Book of Revelation to Ezra Pound's Chinese bathtub, I think. I'm pleased to see the backyards of the small houses just beyond the fence close by over on the left in this part of the cemetery, their trees shading her grave, but it's hard to be here, so while Diane puts the flowers in a vase in front of the stone I wander off to look at some of the other graves. There's a section for children across the little road, stone bunnies on some of the graves, and beyond them moving toward the flags in a big open circle the graves of veterans. I walk past those to see if I can find the marker for my boyhood gymnastics friend, but I can't find it. As I walk back to find Diane, I see my father has pulled up in his Audi. I'm surprised, happy to see him there, unplanned-for like this. He must drive by here every day, Diane says later as we drive over to his house. He has a new cat, an angular orange male my niece found feral in Kentucky on a horse farm. They've named him Kentucky, "KT" for short.

On the Road

I want to say that the anecdote is like the corpse primped up, cotton in its cheeks, fooling nobody it's true to life. But somehow that seems fake, forced, "literary." There is little that is or should be literary about the anecdote. Too much self-consciousness about style is as out of place in the genre as analysis and argument. And yet, as Alain Badiou points out in his fine book on Saint Paul, the gospels are mostly anecdotes cobbled together, while Saint Paul's epistles are something else—militant declarations of a paradigm shift to be recognized by all who would be faithful to the "event." The anecdote is story, the other manifesto framing story. That seems right, I guess. I am all for story but must admit that, for me, anecdote will never be enough. Anyway there is too little seen here, too little understood, and what is understood was understood too late to be of much use. But there's always too little time.

I do know that my leave is only possible because of my job, my work as professor and administrator. If I forgot that for a moment, or if I want to forget it, it is impossible to do that when, out of the blue, I receive an email from Frank Schmit in Luxembourg, telling me that he means to come to Oxford. Frank was my first graduate student and wrote a master's thesis on the history and theory of the avant-garde. Later, after he'd moved home to Luxembourg, he invited me to come over to take part in a defense of the same thesis he had already defended in Oxford. He needed to jump through hoops in front of the local authorities to obtain his teaching certificate. That trip made possible my first visit to Dublin, where I spent time with my first PhD student, Bill Walsh, and his family, and the poets Maurice Scully and Randolph Healy. Bill's brother, or maybe it was Bill himself, managed to get us all tossed from a disco in the wee hours of the morning, and we had one hell of a time, courtesy of the government of Luxembourg and, ultimately, the university system of Ohio. I would have found a way otherwise, but I might as well admit that life as a professor has its moments, not least because the best students often turn out to be friends.

A hard rain does nothing for the humidity, steam rising off pavements, but I decide it's been long enough since Milo and I went out to the park. There's nothing but bad news, the economy is collapsing, and what else is there to do in Oxford? But it's a beautiful sun in the early evening, a low sun, orange enough that I'm reminded that already the days are getting shorter. It's been a wet summer, but some of the weeds are dry and brown along Brown Road. I'm driving the speed limit when from off on the right a bird flies into my vision, landing ten yards in front of me in the middle of the road. There's no stopping, but I don't hit it with my wheels. Instead I hear a noise coming from the underbelly of the car and so look in the rearview mirror. Sure enough, the bird is bouncing on its back on the road behind, dead as a nail. You don't do it over.

OXFORD, OHIO 9/07–6/08

Acknowledgments

Rae Armantrout: "Double" from *Veil: New and Selected Poems* (Wesleyan, 2001), © 2001 by Rae Armantrout; excerpts from "Tease," "*As* (2)," and "Promise" from *Next Life* (Wesleyan, 2007), © 2007 by Rae Armantrout. Reprinted with the permission of Wesleyan University Press.

John Cage: Excerpts from *A Year from Monday* (Wesleyan, 1967). © 1967 by John Cage. Reprinted with the permission of Wesleyan University Press.

cris cheek and Sianed Jones: Excerpt from *songs from navigation* (Reality Street, 1997). © 2007 by cris cheek and Sianed Jones. Reprinted with the permission of the authors.

J. V. Cunningham: "Epigram #21," Epigram #23," and four lines from "Coffee" from *The Poems of J. V. Cunningham*, edited with an introduction and commentary by Timothy Steele (Swallow Press/Ohio University Press, 1997). © 1997 by Jessie Cuningham. Reprinted with the permission of Ohio University Press.

Bill Griffiths: Excerpt from "Reekie" in *Nomad Sense* (Talus Editions, 1998). © 1998 by Bill Griffiths. Reprinted with the permission of Joanne Harman.

Alan Halsey: Excerpt from "Dante's Barber Shop"

mills in Flames (Carcanet, 2010). © 2007, 2010 by Tom Raworth. Reprinted with the permission of the author and Carcanet Press Limited.

Maurice Scully: "A Personal Note" from *Livelihood* (Wild Honey Press, 2004). © 2004 by Maurice Scully. Reprinted by permission of the author.

Lorenzo Thomas: "Downtown Boom," from *Texas in Poetry* 2, ed. Billy Bob Hill (Texas Christian University Press, 2002). © 2002 by Lorenzo Thomas. Reprinted with the permission of Aldon L. Nielsen.

Catherine Wagner: ["God knows questions are beside the point"] in *Everyone in the Room is a Representative of the World at Large* (Bonfire Press, 2007). © 2007 by Catherine Wagner. Reprinted with the permission of the author.

Hannah Weiner: Excerpt from *Weeks* (Xexoxial, 1990). © 1990 by Hannah Weiner. Reprinted with the permission of Charles Bernstein.

John Wilkinson: "The Line of Reinforcement," *Contrivances* (Salt Publishing, 2003). © 2003 by John Wilkinson. Reprinted by permission of the author.

Tyrone Williams, "Tag," from *c.c.* (Krupskaya, 2002). © 2002 by Tyrone Williams. Reprinted by permission of the author.

Thanks also to Brad Blackstone, Justin Katko, Steven Paul Lansky, Patrick Pritchett, Tom Raworth, and Aaren Yandrich for permission to include their emails to the author, and to Nate Dorward, Ken Edwards,

Tony Frazer, Randolph Healy, Rod Smith, Sasha Steensen, Glenn Storhaug, and Rebecca Woolf for help with obtaining permission to reprint some of the poems included here.

Lightning Source UK Ltd.
Milton Keynes UK
UKOW051956010512

191798UK00001B/1/P